Values for
Church Schools

Values for
Church Schools

Peter Shepherd

The National Society
A Christian Voice in Education

a co-publication with
Church House Publishing

National Society/Church House Publishing
Church House
Great Smith Street
London SW1P 3NZ

ISBN 0 901819 61 1

First Published 1998 by The National Society and Church House
Publishing
Second impression 1998

© *The National Society (Church of England) for Promoting
Religious Education 1998*

Acknowledgement

New English Bible © Oxford University Press and Cambridge
University Press 1961, 1970.

Printed by The Cromwell Press Ltd, Trowbridge, Wiltshire

Contents

Preface

'Values in education' is currently in vogue. For a variety of complex socio-political (and possibly even religious) reasons, we approach the Millennium with the cry, 'Teach them some values', ringing in our ears. It is as though values had just been invented! Many of us may, quite understandably, say, 'What have we been doing over the past *x* years, if we've not been teaching values?'

Ah! But have we been doing so with due care and attention? Have we, for example, been so implicit in our teaching, that our values have become lost in the fog of constant curricular revision (like the so-called 'hidden curriculum', which was sometimes so well hidden, it was difficult to discern at all.)? Have we ever considered making our teaching of values much more explicit? What is clear enough, is that there is now a mood in the country to bring values to the forefront of educational debate. Whether this is for the best of reasons: formal recognition – at last – that we cannot possibly educate children in a values vacuum, or whether it is due more to political expediency or, again, to some kind of popular gut-reaction that something is wrong with the state of the nation, can only be, from our present perspective, a matter of opinion. The point is that, at last, those concerned with values in education are being heeded. The 'time to speak'[1] has arrived.

But what of our Church schools? Are we content to let the secular world set our agenda? Are we heck, as we (southerners) say in the north! We Christians are called to be in the world, but not simply of it. If our Church schools are to be distinctive – and I believe that if they are not, there is no point in having them – then those values which are intrinsic to our school communities, and which we also seek to transmit via the curriculum, must be equally distinctive. What follows is just one person's attempt to identify and elucidate them.

Peter Shepherd
All Saints Tide 1997

vii

What is a value?

The term 'value', finding its root in the Latin '*valere*', 'to be strong' or 'to be worth',[1] represents that which we hold ultimately to be most dear. Originally, it was used to refer solely to economic worth, and so it is no accident that the word 'dear' is applied today to that which has high monetary value. A broadening out of the concept in the nineteenth century may be particularly identified with the work of philosophers such as Lotze and Ritschl (the latter a significant Protestant theologian). Nietzsche, who was to declare that 'God is dead', argued that people were free to create their own values, and went on to propound the notion of the '*ubermensch*', those 'supermen' who would impose their will on the weak and valueless! The first work in English on the subject, 'Valuation, Its Nature and Laws', was published by an American, Wilbur Urban, in 1909. So we should not be surprised when John E. Smith, in the relevant article in SCM's *Dictionary of Christian Ethics*,[2] points out that 'value' is a 'modern term'. It has, furthermore, been 'used to indicate what traditionally has gone by the name of "good" or "the good"'. This judgement is helpfully developed by Iris Murdoch:

> 'Value' does not belong inside the world of truth functions, the world of science and factual propositions. So it must live somewhere else. It is then attached somehow to the human will, a shadow clinging to a shadow... but since will is pure choice, pure movement, and not thought or vision, will really requires only action words such as 'good' or 'right'.[3]

The focus of a value ought, then, to be 'for the good'. But surely there may be values which are not? Or rather, it may be that a particular value turns out to be so focused on one's own good, that it is antipathetic to the good of others. Almost paradoxically,

1

therefore, some values – the good and the right – may actually be neither good nor right. The implications of the *'ubersmensch'* whatever Nietzsche might have had in mind, were not lost on Hitler![4] To make this point is to recognise an important element of subjectivity in any debate about values, simply because what is held to be worthy may well vary from person to person. For:

> if the life-world is at every point always seen in terms of values, if valuation is first of all, then values do not need objective grounding... They may be assessed and criticised, or in various ways selectively developed, trained and redirected... [for] we are always already within a culture, that is an organisation and a transformation of the values of life. History has already bequeathed to us, embodied in our current language and practices, an interpretation of life or a second-level evaluation of life.[5]

Values are not formed in a vacuum. There will be a host of 'givens', such as our history, our culture and, of course, our systems of belief by and through which we interpret the world, and our place in it. These will exert enormous influence on the development of any one person's set of values. It is perfectly possible, perhaps even to be expected, that we will find lives being lived according to values which some may deplore, but which others believe to be quite unexceptionable, e.g. the pursuit of wealth for its own sake. People will not only disagree over the relative weighting to be given to any particular value, but it may even be that what we once considered important may diminish in significance with new insights and new experiences.

The problem with values

For the reasons mentioned above, any discussion of allegedly 'common values' is very difficult. On what basis can anyone claim with confidence that such and such a value should be accepted by all? How far can there ever be true consensus without a common myth, shared ideology or some other kind of agreed belief system? Even the value that we place on human life, which we might expect to be axiomatic (a truth *worthy* of acceptance), has not always been universally shared in the past, and is clearly not shared by all today: just consider the human rights records of some countries, or the varying views on capital punishment. But even when we move away from significant issues on which we might (arguably) expect some degree of agreement, to those (equally arguably) more debatable values, such as whether boys and girls should be educated separately, or whether monogamy is an absolute human condition, or a relative and culturally determined value, then we find ourselves in a minefield.

We may like to think that the things we value most highly are bound to be valued equally highly by everyone else. When we find that is not the case, we may feel despair: 'are there no absolutes, or is there no objectivity to be found anywhere?' Perhaps the answer must be: 'not in this world',[1] a world characterized by so much diversity of ideology and such varied history and culture and a century marked by 'the collapse of traditional truths and ultimate horrors',[2] that it is impossible to find much common ground. An age of scientific relativity has brought with it a cultural, philosophical and theological relativity; the uncertainty principle has deified uncertainty; and chaos has become a respected theory. So, we may conclude, values are belief-driven, attitudinal and fundamentally subjective.

That is not the only problem. So far it may have been assumed that we have been dealing purely with moral value. Not so:

> Despite a long tradition which identified all questions concerning the good for man as a goal, or individual goods involved in particular situations, as 'ethical' questions, the aim behind the development of a general theory of value is to characterise value in its *generic* sense.[3]

In other words, there are different kinds of value, one form only being *moral value*. In 1926 a groundbreaking study by Ralph Perry, *A General Theory of Value*, identified 'realms' of value including religion, art, science, politics, law and custom, as well as economics and morality. Since then philosophers have discussed the distinction between instrumental and intrinsic value (i.e. means and ends), technical, contributory or final value, as well as the relationship of value to fact (leading to theories on the objectivity of value and value judgements). So the study of value is massive and complex. What is clear enough, in this jungle of ideas, is that there is no compelling need to identify the meaning of 'good' with one value or one value system alone, and reject all other meanings. Nor, indeed, should we leave the term with no meaning at all, as some would have us do ('a vacuous concept – forget it!'). What we do need is clarity in the way we employ the various ideas associated with 'value'.

Can we speak of 'foundation values'?

In the present educational debate, particularly that focused on, and perhaps inspired by, the School Curriculum and Assessment Authority (SCAA),[1] which established the National Forum for Values in Education and the Community, the meaning of 'value' often seems assumed to have mainly, or even purely, moral connotations: to do with how we behave, or more precisely, how we ought, or ought not to behave. So, for example, an article written about this debate by the Archbishop of Canterbury,[2] was headlined, 'Morals are made in the classroom'. This was followed by John Leary's article, 'Added moral value',[3] which purported to describe 'the shifting positions in the latest debate', but found only 'a statement that represented a consensus on *moral* values'.[4] Undoubtedly, such a focus is both 'worthy' and 'valuable', but a debate about values must be more than just a debate about issues of morality, as important as they are. It is particularly important to understand this when those engaged in the SCAA exercise are, after all, trying to provide support for schools in promoting pupils' '*spiritual,* moral, *social* and *cultural* development'.[5]

At the very least there is a worrying lack of clarity surrounding the debate. Any trawl of the educational press would discover that without too much trouble.[6] While reference will be made to SMSC, the S, S and C are often then, to all intents and purposes, quietly ignored. Even the Church press has interpreted the debate in this narrow fashion: the headline 'Minister worried by values' moved directly into: 'A draft code on teaching morality in schools'.[7] If 'morality' is being used as a shorthand term to cover and embrace other values, then its use is particularly confusing. That may be irritating, but irritation is less important than the possibility that constant misuse of language will lead people to assume that the pursuit of 'values in education' is, after all, only about teaching codes of behaviour. Tell them not to graffiti the toilets, and they'll stop doing it! The problem is, as history makes clear, that codes handed out on 'tablets of stone', without proper embedding in a system of belief, are just not heeded. Even when they are so embedded, as the Law given to the Israelites,[8] they cannot prevent a fall into idolatry![9]

So the values debate needs to be multi-dimensional:

> Axiological ethics does not focus directly on what we should do. Instead it centres on questions of what is worth pursuing or promoting and what should be avoided... Much modern discussion of values has treated them in the context of our deciding what things to have or not to have in our lives.[10]

Without linking morality with other, more basic value systems, there is a danger that the debate, as it affects teaching and learning, may become sterile. Even when responding to the very proper demand (articulated for the nation by the widow of murdered Head, Philip Lawrence) that we should work to 'heal our fractured society',[11] to focus then only on matters to do with behaviour, without considering those values and other beliefs which impinge on behaviour, means that an otherwise essential debate will almost inevitably become shallow and ultimately short-lived.

If we make an analogy with house building, we might say that there are fundamental and basic 'foundation values', on which any values debate must be built. These should be clear enough in a religious context – do we not sing 'Christ is our cornerstone'?[12] – and there are others which may be articulated and explored by those so committed in other contexts. While this booklet is not the place to develop this latter exercise, we may note in passing that Christian non-realism has found it a fertile field for redrawing the Christian map. Cupitt, for example, discusses a variety of approaches towards developing the foundations of a non-religious system of values.[13]

So there are basic or generic values. Are these ideals or articles of faith or...? Whatever they are,[14] they lie behind more specific areas of value (moral, social, etc.). If we forget the former, we will not get very far with the latter. We need good foundations and cornerstones to give shape and substance to the building. We can then say, 'This is what we stand for'. Such values may even be what we are prepared to die for. Whatever else, they provide the context from within which we operate, and so are (to change the metaphor) the central points of reference for our lives. Quite simply they are those qualities or convictions which we hold to be most dear, most worthy and most right. There is nothing penultimate about them. But what are they?

The search for the holy grail

It may be argued that these basic or core values are, in fact, spiritual,[1] although in the educational debate, a failure to find completely adequate definitions of spirituality has not helped this particular exploration to move forward. If morality and spirituality are confused, it would be equally mistaken to identify spiritual values purely with religion: there is much spirituality to be found outside religions. Just to muddy the waters further, there is also an unhelpful correlation between values and beliefs.[2] Are they the same? As we shall see, a similar problem pertains to the relationship between belief and faith. It may be that if we can untie that knot, we may be able to see our way to untying the other. But in terms of SMSC, we need to hold firm to Alan Brown's advice, 'If the "spiritual" is properly and fully addressed, the "moral, social and cultural" will fall into place more easily.'[3]

There is a further problem. In a society that is both secular and multi-faith, efforts to determine a common core of 'foundation' values, without having a common context in which to do so, are most likely to lead to a blandness – a truly low common denominator that is next to useless because, in seeking not to offend anyone, it helps no-one at all. The way that the SCAA exercise treated marriage is a case in point. The bizarre way in which SCAA sought the views of religious groups is another. But no debate on values which fails to take proper account of the critique of religious (or non-religious) faiths will ever be entirely satisfactory. In religious terms, for example, some secular values might be criticized as idolatrous (in that they put 'things' above God – who may be thought of as Ultimate Value) or demonic (in that they enable distortions and perversions to enter human life). Perhaps the problem is that so much recent curriculum debate, unlike that of HMI during the late 1970s (which many of us remember with fondness) has been based rather more in political ideology than in any understanding of the nature of personhood. These comments are not meant to be unsympathetic towards or overly critical of those who have taken on this challenge. We should be particularly grateful to SCAA and OFSTED for their groundbreaking work encouraging schools to grapple with SMSC.

So the Values Forum has been commissioned to find the holy grail: a common set of values for our country, which can then be embedded in the educational system. Has that grail been found? A set of agreed values was indeed announced in May 1996, and further work has been, and continues to be done on them. In the summer of 1997 a draft values document was published to a limited audience, with a view to nation-wide distribution at a future date. Although articulate and thought-provoking, some may consider that it is trying to teach the proverbial ancestor to suck hens' ovulations (in the sense that we will all sign up to be 'for' tolerance and respect, just as we are all 'against' sin), and we may also find it not easily translatable into day-to-day, teacher-friendly, classroom practice, 'Much of the advice is wordy, and some is woolly as well. Some is also patronising to head teachers. Do they really not know already that they should praise pupils for genuine effort and achievement?'[4]

It is of particular interest, and to be welcomed, that the draft document does not ignore spirituality, despite the press perspectives noted above. Nevertheless, the approach is ultimately confined, and so confining.[5] The understanding shown of the role of RE itself is regrettably narrow, and the contribution of the wider curriculum to pupils' values education seems not to have been sufficiently recognized. As might be expected, in seeking to deal with the vast range of spiritual experience and insight represented in this country, let alone that of mankind as a whole, any common view is bound to be partial and, in seeking to avoid too much disagreement, will fail to inspire.

So we must accept that any values debate of worth (or value!) will tread a difficult path. Perhaps we should not be surprised if, when we think we have the grail, what we have really found is just another piece of a growing curricular tea service – very useful, but certainly not the end of the quest. Values are the qualities and attributes on which lives are based and lived. As such they are the implicit, if not explicit, context of our intentions and desires; they are fundamental in determining our opinions. Perhaps any attempt to produce a set of values that all will accept is doomed from the start in any case. Values are just too important.

What of Anglican schools?

We ought not to have that problem, or not that degree of problem, within our Anglican schools. At least we know what we stand for – don't we? We may surely assume that Church schools will wish to share those common behavioural (moral) values which would be espoused by any good school, such as care for others, fair play, tolerance, etc. But any serious consideration of a values statement for our schools must go much further than that, and must be undertaken from an explicitly Christian perspective. This may (or may not) end up by being quite different from those arising from a Muslim, Buddhist or Humanist perspective. That should not worry us. Why become agitated over difference? Why aim for dull uniformity? It is only by discussing our differences that we may learn from each other. So our particular quest is the identification of values that are specifically Christian, and which we should not necessarily assume to be commonly held. Indeed such values may not be recognised,[1] or may even be derided[2] or resisted[3] by the world. They will probably not be the kinds of matters which secular committees or forums debating values in education would ever consider.

What are Christian values?

Certain values are essential to the life of a Christian community, and to personal and corporate growth in that community. While recognizing the element of subjectivity in any values debate, we may go so far as to say that for a Christian community, such as a

9

Church school, these values ought to be considered non-negotiable and absolute, i.e. faith imperatives, which the very nature of our Christian tradition and experience gives us no choice but to accept. This is not to suggest that the values explored in this booklet are exhaustive of the Christian tradition! Indeed, the more discussion I had with colleagues, the more I realized just how many equally important values I had omitted to consider. However, a line had to be drawn somewhere, and so the selection below simply includes those values which, from my perspective and in my experience, are the most central for any Christian school community. I have no doubt that the reader will say, 'He has missed out *x*. Isn't *y* crucial?' Of course I have, and of course they are! However, I would venture to suggest that whatever else school governing bodies consider ought to inform their own values statement, Church schools which do not take these particular values seriously are in danger of not fully understanding, and so possibly not fulfilling their vocation in either ministry or in mission. Readers will have to judge for themselves just how far this claim is reasonable.

The importance of 'God-talk'

The approach will seek to combine both the theological and the spiritual. We need 'God-talk' because we cannot seriously reflect on our faith without it. This special kind of thinking will seldom be straightforward, particularly for those who may be unaccustomed to engaging with it, but it is essential if we are to clarify the connection between our faith and our work as teachers and governors. Some of the values considered below are quite mind-stretching, but I express the hope that my initial discussion of them will facilitate your own.

We also need to operate on a more than purely cerebral or academic level: we must dig deeply into our spiritual resources as well. Only in so doing can we hope to plumb the depths of what is ultimately valuable. So educational debate in our Church schools must be prayer-full. As Evagrius, one of the Desert Fathers, put it, 'A theologian is one whose prayer is true. If you truly pray, you are a theologian.'[1] There is a vital connection in any Christian debate between the spiritual and the theological:

> Christian spirituality makes it possible for the theologian to breathe theologically. Theological reason... is part of a larger trinitarian conversation. The 'breath' of this con-versation – even of the meaningful pauses, which are more like outbursts of adoration – is what authentic Christian spirituality inhales. And it is what theology seeks to inhale when it turns to this kind of spirituality. But our inhaling is the other and 'smaller' side of a greater 'exhaling'. And that seems to be why theological *logos* is the tip of a much greater *doxology*.[2]

The model of the 'larger trinitarian conversation' is truly inspira-tional. As we search to express our faith, we may come to believe that our conversation and our debates are held within the deepest 'recesses' (if you will pardon the crudeness of this particular expression) of God. That at one and the same time that we are thinking 'theologically' (*'logoi...theos'* may be usefully para-phrased 'words about God'), we are also engaging in 'words of praise/glory' (*'logoi... doxa'*). We may even, on too few occasions no doubt, but as the psalmist recommended, pause and be still.[3]

> Wisdom calls this hectic generation to attend to one thing at a time. She teaches a deep attention, with a heart willing to receive, quiet, turning from self. The gates are to be thrown open that the radiance of the eternal spirit may come in and make its home.[4]

We might simply say that there are times to 'shut up and listen' (Koheleth 'The Preacher' made the same point rather more felici-tously!)[5]

Any serious consideration of values within a Christian context must therefore have not only the intellectual rigour that theology requires, but also the spiritual discernment that enables those theological insights to 'breathe'. After all, '[The] Spirit is the "breath" of all that we are, especially our minds and hearts. A "pneumonia of the mind" is a critical sign that the Spirit's gifts are not yet fully appreciated.'[6] The *pneumon* (lung) is obviously closely related to the pneuma, which is 'spirit', 'breath' and 'wind'.[7] The disease may be physical or spiritual; and who is to say which is the worst kind? This exploration is one that will, I hope, encourage the school community to breathe together healthily in every sense, for if we truly live these values, the life of the school, and of those who belong to it, can only improve.

On the values journey

As with any proper exploration we need map and compass. Our Christian map can only be the Bible, which gives access to the classic revelatory sources of our faith. Scripture provides both stability and continuity for our Christian community. Each of the values under discussion will therefore begin with a biblical 'prompt'. But we also need a compass to guide our path as we use the map, and that must be the developed, and developing, traditions of the Church. Traditions are literally those things which are 'handed down'[1] and which transmit God's revelation alongside, and even sometimes prior to, our Scriptures.[2] One of the main functions of tradition is that of interpretation, and it is clear that if we are to make our faith real to growing minds, it must be reinterpreted for every generation.

Of course, in so doing we have to apply ourselves to the process and, quite frankly, be prepared to use our God-given brains, provided we recognize our limitations:

At the centre of the Christian faith stands Jesus Christ. His personality, as presented by Scripture and Tradition, at once historical and actual and, while of earth, far surpassing all things earthly, is not to be taken in by the human mind at one glance.[3]

So we will humbly bring our reason to the task. But, as will be clearly detected, I, personally, have no interest in any faith that is not fundamentally reasonable. In this I have at least William Temple on my side![4]

Finally, our journey would be disastrous if we each simply go our own way, plotting whatever route we think best, so we need some authoritative voices (which I suppose are an aspect of the tradition, but worth distinguishing analogically from the compass, perhaps as guidebooks) to which we can turn for help should we get lost. It is also important that we do not lose sight of where we are; and so each section will seek to locate its discussion in the only place it can be held – in school. Neither theology nor prayer should feel out of place in a Church school, even though we may sometimes feel much more comfortable with the latter than with the former!

This point is important. There will, therefore, be a number of questions asked at the beginning of each section, some of which may be more relevant to governors, others to professional practitioners. It is to be hoped that at least some of the questions will engage governors and teachers in discussion together. Schools may wish to consider how far particular values have implications for policy and practice, and so may be encouraged to use their reflections as a basis for self-evaluation in every aspect of the school's life: curriculum, the management of teaching and learning, worship, discipline and so on. In fact, everything that is valuable in our work.

You will see that I have somewhat artificially distinguished between values which may be best transmitted via the curriculum, and those values which ought to be intrinsic to the school, and therefore a part of the living, breathing, praying community.

It may be that some would prefer to relocate a particular value to the other section. It is more likely to be the case that, in making any such distinction, we are simply looking at the same values from different perspectives (a prime example is 'concern for truth'). I have also tried to focus on values which are interconnected, so that the booklet may be read as a coherent and structured whole. Indeed, I have found it virtually impossible to consider any one of the values I have identified, without also considering its connection with at least one of the others. Sometimes whole 'banks' of these values have impinged upon my writing, so that they just could not be ignored. You may well find the same. Whatever: breathe in and be with God, who is ultimately *axios*:

> Thou art worthy, O Lord our God, to receive glory and honour and power, because thou didst create all things; by thy will they were created and have their being![5]

Christian values
within the curriculum

Awe, wonder and fascination

When I look up at thy heavens, the work of thy fingers, the moon and the stars set in place by thee, what is man...? (Psalm 8.3-4)

FOR DISCUSSION:

1. *Are awe and wonder to be found in every area of your school's curriculum?*

2. *Should we engage our younger pupils in an exploration of the mystery of evil?*

3. *How can we encourage our pupils to stop, stand and stare?*

4. *Is the mystery of God conveyed in our worship?*

5. *What is the place of 'the Holy' in our curriculum?*

6. *How can we as adults recover our 'childlike' sense of wonder?*

7. *Rudolf Otto invited his readers to direct their minds 'to a moment of deeply-felt religious experience'. Can teachers and governors establish a 'wonder-full' curriculum for the benefit of the pupils?*

In our teaching of the sciences and geography we want children to come to see the natural world and the universe around us, not as the impersonal machine that it is often made to appear, but as a purposeful context for life. Such understanding ought to inspire feelings of awe and wonder in us. In this we share the age-old human propensity to be dwarfed and surprised, just as the psalmist was. As we reflect on that verse from Psalm 8, can we not imagine the poet staring up into the sky, his mind 'boggling'? 'How large it all is; and how small I am.' Have you ever stood out on a starry night, looked up, and allowed your imagination to take flight? Just think how far away is the nearest 'heavenly' object (the moon), the nearest planet, the nearest star; and how long ago they were formed. There are some truly awe-inspiring mathematics on time-scales and distances to be done with the children! We can particularly learn from those who have been privileged to see it from the other side:

> Suddenly from behind the rim of the moon, in long, slow-motion moments of immense majesty, there emerges a sparkling blue and white jewel, a light, delicate sky-blue sphere laced with slowly swirling veils of white, rising gradually like a small pearl in a thick sea of black mystery. It takes more than a moment to fully realise this is Earth...home.[1]

There are some wonderful photographs available of 'the heavens' which can touch the child in all of us.[2]

Theologically, such an experience is well-expressed by Rudolf Otto's concept of God as the 'mysterium tremendum' – that 'numinous presence' [which] overwhelms', and also fascinates and draws.[3] The notion of transcendence (which is what we are concerned with here) connotes the unimaginable and the unthink-able. To experience the summons of the Transcendent is to experience the ultimate, the very limit of our being, and will necessarily inspire dread. But that dread, fearful in itself, is simply the beginning of awe and wonder:

> for the dark infinity which threatens to engulf us is the infinity out of which we came and which promises to renew our being as creatures of infinity.[4]

So one theologian reflects on the ecological crisis facing humankind. Left to itself, and seen from a purely human perspective, the future of our planet often seems awful; from the perspective of eternity, it can be awe-full. Which perspective is more likely to encourage us to do something about it?

This is clearly a situation when it is entirely appropriate to use the term 'mystery', referring not simply to something we do not understand (a secret or riddle which we may work out, like Hercule Poirot using his 'little grey cells'), but something that is always *beyond*, because it is 'of God'. While Christian faith is not a 'mystery religion', nevertheless we do claim some access to God's 'mysterious' purposes through revelation in Jesus Christ.[5] The teacher in a Church school will at least prepare pupils to explore this mystery to some extent. In an age in which technology has become the philosopher's stone of the curriculum, we may be tempted to feel that all the mystery is disappearing from our lives. Just press the right buttons and all our problems will be solved! It is even more important, therefore, that we enable our children to understand that technology is a tool, and not (as some may try to persuade us) an end in itself.

> Transcendence needs to be taken up into the stream of imaginative imagery and song and music which in our electronic age pervasively mould the dispositions and attitude to life of very many people. The application to life must be the work of people creative in the arts of all kinds, including the art of living, responding to their experience

17

of Transcendence and embodying it in the concrete mythic forms in terms of which human life is lived.[6]

While it is reasonable for us to regard 'the Mystery' as of God, we must not fall into the error of assuming that the two are simply synonymous. In a book actually entitled *The Tremendum*, Arthur Cohen, arguing that the only way to address the experience of the Holocaust is through silence, takes Otto's concept one stage further:

> [I have] no language with which to speak of evil...[and so have] constructed a modern theology without dealing with evil... as *'tremendum'*. I call the death camps the *'tremendum'*, for it is the monument of a meaningless inversion of life to an orgiastic celebration of death, to a psychosexual and pathological degeneracy unparalleled and unfathomable to any person bonded to life.[7]

We might even say that for the twentieth century one of the greatest and most unfathomable mysteries is what has been called the 'silence of God' over the Holocaust.[8] While that kind of exploration might seem to be a tall order for primary schools, secondary pupils may well be ready to wrestle with this particular *tremendum*.

In more general terms, although 'dread' is not the obvious candidate to be recommended for school life, children are potentially more able than adults to feel dwarfed, or even threatened. Not simply because they are small in stature and knowledge, although that very real, and sometimes frightening experience can offer genuine perspective, but because they have greater openness than the more fully-formed adult to the wonder and mystery of things. There are, of course, those mature people who have not lost the ability to rejoice like little children:

> As I move about in the sunshine I feel in the midst of the supernatural; in the midst of immortal things. It is impos-

sible to wrest the mind down to the same laws that rule pieces of timber, water or earth. They do not control the soul, however rigidly they may bind matter.[9]

But one of the saddest things imaginable is the cynical child; the one who has seen it all; the one who cannot be surprised. For example, while there may be other reasons to question the introduction of Father Christmas to young, impressionable minds, there will always be a hint of regret when the child comes to realize that Santa isn't real: all the more so when s/he is told by some other streetwise peer. For when all the mystery is removed from our lives, we are the poorer. We often hear the saying, 'Don't let them grow up too fast'. What wise words! If the teacher can keep this awareness of mystery and wonder so alive that it follows us into adult life, then a real educational task has been achieved.

Humility

Then Job answered the Lord: 'I know that thou canst do all things and that no purpose is beyond thee. But I have spoken of great things which I have not understood, things too wonderful for me to know. I knew of thee then only by report, but now I see with my own eyes. Therefore I melt away; I repent in dust and ashes.' (Job 42.1-6)

Once we have experienced the wonder of our universe we begin to see (as many scientists are now saying quite openly) that we may never have all the answers. Paul Davies, (the title of his book echoing the final – probably tongue-in-cheek – sentence of Hawking's well-sold, but little-read, classic[1]) makes the point clearly:

> I have always wanted to believe that science can explain everything, at least in principle. Most religions demand belief in at least some supernatural events, which are by definition impossible to reconcile with science. Although I obviously can't prove that they never happen, I see no reason to suppose that they do. But even if one rules out supernatural events, it is still not clear that science could in principle explain everything in the physical universe. Sooner or later we all have to accept something as given, whether it is God or logic, or a set of laws, or some other foundation for existence. Thus 'ultimate' questions will always lie beyond the scope of empirical science as it is usually defined.[2]

It was also a hard lesson for Job to learn; it took the loss of everything he held dear (everything he 'valued') for him to realise that what he had always felt so sure about, i.e. the extent to which he had 'sussed it all out', just wasn't the case at all. Theologically, of course, we are not speaking here of empirical knowledge, but of his understanding of the way that God operates (the Job story is a theodicy – an attempt to reconcile the righteousness of God with the reality of evil and suffering). The author of Job makes the point clearly enough that there are no absolute answers. That when it comes to things of God we can only grope, so to speak, in the dark, relying on what light there may be. Job's answer (above) was the only response that could be made to the magisterial 'Where were you when I laid the earth's foundations?'[3]

Such intellectual humility is the sign of a truly educated person. How often have we read of scholars who 'wear their learning lightly'? But it is not simply about having great knowledge. It is pre-eminently about understanding our human condition, and responding appropriately; about knowing our place, and coming to terms with it. It is what the existentialist philosophers call living an 'authentic existence'.

The process of education may be understood (taking some liberties with the Latin root[4]) to be all about 'leading out'. Taking a child and leading her out onto the road to authentic, autonomous and responsible adulthood; as (we say) a 'human being'. In fact, I want to go one step further. I have often regarded our self-description as human 'beings' (if we understand 'being' to connote a static condition) as presumptuous arrogance! Perhaps we might find more humility in the notion of a human 'becoming'?[5] We are not there yet; we are pilgrims on the way; we are moving towards our potential and our destiny. Education for humility will inevitably be a cross-curricular experience, because it will cover the whole range of what it means to be truly human, and out of it should arise a respect for the ideas of others.

Concern for the truth

When he comes who is the Spirit of truth, he will guide you into all the truth...and the truth will set you free. (John 16.13; 8.33)

FOR DISCUSSION:

1. *Question: 'Do you like my new bike?' Answer: 'It's not as good/expensive as mine.' Should we teach our children that they should always tell the truth, no matter what? If there is to be a line, where should it be drawn?*

2. *How much truth should we tell on parents' evenings? Is honesty always the best policy?*

3. *Can we risk always answering children's questions truthfully, or are there times to prevaricate?*

4. *What criteria can we develop to enable us to deal with the Bible truthfully (but not necessarily literally)?*

5. *Are certain truths more appropriate for certain age groups?*

' "What is truth?" said jesting Pilate; and would not stay for an answer.'[1] Quite understandable, really, for the answer would have been as difficult for him as it is for us all. The Greek *aletheia* connotes 'unhiddenness' or 'unconcealment'; that which is laid bare when the accretions which cover it are stripped off. Rather like peeling the skin from an onion; eventually you arrive at the core. Theologically we are on safe ground in recognizing truth as a supreme Christian value; after all, Jesus Christ is not only full of it,[2] he is it.[3] For Gandhi – the great-souled one – Truth was God.[4] But when it comes to facing the reality of truth, we may, like Pilate, find other things to do. Sometimes the truth is hard for us, and hard on us. Having things, or at least certain things, laid bare is often uncomfortable. Nevertheless, as Christians we are called to take truth with the utmost seriousness: God's Spirit is the Spirit of Truth, and only by accepting that can we be truly free. To do otherwise is, presumably, to be in bondage to the 'father of lies'![5] Here we might usefully reflect on the text which has caused great worry to many Christians down the ages: just what is the unforgivable sin (and have I committed it?)[6] If the Holy Spirit is the bringer of truth, then to sin against the Holy Spirit is to treat as false that which we know is true, 'This is the unpardonable sin, not because God is ever unwilling to pardon a penitent, but because an inner dishonesty makes a man incapable of that honest appraisal of himself which is repentance.'[7] To deny the truth is to separate oneself from the ultimately valuable.

It goes almost without saying that our Church schools must be communities of truth, and that commitment to truth must be reflected throughout the curriculum. So pathways will be followed (as far as possible) without fear as to where they may ultimately lead. Children will learn from their study of history and religion that what they might previously have believed to have been 'facts', are actually interpretations of human experience. That concept is, unfortunately, a real mystery for many Christians, who cannot conceive that when they are reading the Bible (for example) they are already engaged in an act of interpretation. As a parent once told me as he was expounding 'what the Bible said' about the spiritual dangers of studying Shakespeare, 'What you say is interpretation; what I say is The Truth'!

Our children must learn that, in order to interpret, we have to allow the evidence to speak to us. Sometimes the evidence may seem to undermine our dearest beliefs. Being 'led out' on the road of 'human becoming' requires us to follow wherever the evidence leads us, as hard as that might occasionally be, because just as 'thirst was made for water; enquiry [was made] for truth'.[8] That

23

is not to recommend a thorough-going relativism (i.e. all ideas are equally true – it just depends on your perspective), because the truly educated person will still debate what s/he is led to call 'true', forcefully, yet with love and concern for those with whom s/he is debating. But we will try to understand why others see things differently from us and, with that understanding will seek to explore truth together.

Within the school community as well, truth will be valued. Children will be taught the importance of truth-telling, and teachers will learn that it is important not to duck the truth when discussing the child with the parents. There are often hard lessons here. It is sometimes not easy to tell the truth. What if the truth actually causes hurt? If we really believe that the truth does liberate, then we would appear to have little choice. If children learn to tell 'white lies' it is a short step to the other kind. If they can be assured both implicitly and explicitly in their learning that the teacher may be relied upon to tell them the truth whatever, then this will enable them to gain that habit. But I can see the problems in a primary classroom, 'Where does Santa live?' or 'Where is granddad now?' (he has died). No-one ever said that education was easy!

Having asserted the primary imperative for truth, can we not also say that there will be occasions, especially with young children, when we cannot tell the truth 'unvarnished'? Whatever we might want to say about granddad, or indeed, whatever we may personally believe about the post-mortem state, a simple survey of the varying Christian expressions of hope (let alone those of other faiths), some of which appear to be mutually contradictory, demonstrates clearly enough the simple truth that we *just do not know* exactly 'what has happened' to granddad. In this case, it is surely perfectly acceptable to ask the fundamental question, 'Is this an occasion when the truth ('We don't exactly know, but we believe...') might cause distress?' While it is right to express the truth (or at least our conviction of what we believe the truth to be), we must do so in a way that will 'build and plant' rather than 'uproot and destroy'.[9]

While truth is an essential value, so (as we shall see) is love the most central value of all. The former must therefore be tempered with the latter. So there is a risk in being honest! But that is a good lesson to learn in itself.

Possibility

[Naomi said to Ruth] 'Your sister-in-law has gone back to her people and her gods; go back with her'. 'Do not urge me to go back and desert you,' Ruth answered. 'Where you go, I will go.' (Ruth 1.15)

FOR DISCUSSION:

1. *How can we help pupils make the best of what they are and what they have?*

2. *How can pupils best learn about and manage failure?*

3. *How can we help pupils determine what is, and is not, possible for them?*

4. *Does our teaching foster the taking of decisions?*

5. *Do we challenge and encourage pupils to embark upon the adventure of faith?*

The secular world sometimes seems to signal 'that everything is possible'. All you need to do to become rich, my son/daughter, is to work hard! Achievement is always within reach. Certainly life is full of potentialities; but there are 'mights-not' as well as 'mights'. While we may make certain decisions as we journey through life, we just as often have decisions taken for us – by circumstances (birth, wealth, intelligence, and so on) and by accidents which affect those circumstances (the deaths of loved ones, being here instead of there, etc.). In other words, it is our abiding Christian duty to value the reality of possibility; but we will not do so if we believe in limitless possibility. It is simply not true to tell our children that everything is possible; indeed, it may be cruel to do so, for failure is an ever-present reality. Sometimes our areas of freedom may be severely constrained.

The child who is constantly made to feel that s/he could have done better had s/he only tried a little harder, when in fact they have made every effort, and the result is a genuine reflection of that, is already damaged. All we can expect from our pupils is their best, and we also damage them if we do not require that! It may be that for them, that particular possibility (gaining such and such a score in an exam) is just not possible.

So we should value 'possibility' for what it is. God's possibilities may not provide unrestricted opportunity, but they do (unless you are irredeemably deterministic and believe that God has already planned out everything that happens) provide real opportunity and some genuine, albeit not unlimited freedom. Ruth made a choice. Some may have considered it unwise, but she recognised that there are all sorts of possibilities ready for the making. To make the best of opportunity when it arises, children need to value the possibility that it is there at all, but must not take it for granted.

The corollary of this is that we must also value the need to take responsible decisions. With so many possibilities before us, it is quite tempting to 'sit on the fence'. The curriculum must engender the development of decision-making skills. While we might not always make the best decisions, it is probably worse to make none at all. In particular our RE curriculum should present, in appropriate ways, the challenge of religious commitment. This is not to fall into confessionalism. Even in our Church schools we should not use our privileged positions as teachers of religion to evangelize. Nevertheless, it is appropriate to commend serious consideration in the lives of our pupils of the religious perspective, and so the making of some kind of decision about it. The greatest sadness is not when they make decisions that are different from their parents and teachers, but when we have failed to engage them in the process at all:

> Once to every man and nation comes the moment to decide, in the strife of Truth with Falsehood, for the good or evil side.[1]

Rationality

> Then God said, 'Let us make man in our own image and likeness.'(Genesis 1.26)
>
> 'So the Word became flesh...' (John 1.14)

FOR DISCUSSION:

1. *Does our Religious Education programme enable our pupils to enquire rationally into matters of faith?*

2. *In what ways might our teaching create a positive vision of ourselves and our pupils as being 'in the image of God'?*

3. *How can the school deal with irrationality when exhibited by children, parents or staff?*

4. *Is it possible for God's Word to shine through our curriculum? How does this occur?*

5. *Does our curriculum take 'being human' seriously, and reverently, enough?*

Just as destructive as 'everything is possible': a modern curriculum may imply that 'humanity is entirely rational'. As The Beatles sang, 'We can work it out'. 'Problem-solving' is (rightly) in vogue, but overdue emphasis on our ability to solve all our problems may take our rationality so much for granted, that we cease to value it at all. It ought, in any case, to be a matter of simple observation that our alleged rationality is often in short supply; that human beings can be most irrational on occasions! Yes – we do have the ability to judge and discriminate, to sift evidence and evaluate it; we do use interpretative methods, though not always well. Part of the problem is that while we spend enormous amounts of time and energy seeking to find the right answers, we only too often blight that exploration by asking the wrong questions or, rather, by not fully understanding what the right questions might be. In Douglas Adams' radio comedy, philosophers want to know the answer to 'the Great Question', and are offered the answer 'forty-two'!

> 'I checked it very thoroughly', said the computer, 'and that quite definitely is the answer. I think the problem, to be quite honest with you, is that you've never actually known what the question is'. 'But it was the Great Question! The Ultimate Question of Life, the Universe and Everything...'. 'Yes', said Deep Thought with the air of one who suffers fools gladly, 'but what actually *is* it?'[1]

Unless we ask the right questions, we will never find the right answers. That is a lesson every child is entitled to learn. In many, often simple, ways, we do not always know why we do particular things or go in particular directions, and so we move in error as much as in truth. Unless our children recognize the potential for our irrationality to disrupt, not only our lives, but the lives of other people, we will not value our rationality for what it is: in a '*Logos Christology*',[2] nothing other than the 'image of God'. So while rationality may not often be achievable, it is there in its potentiality. Early Christian writers argued that the fact that man is rational ('*logikos*') is a reflection of the divine Word ('*logos*') working in us.

It is clear that St John had both Greek and Hebrew ideas in mind when he chose to describe Jesus Christ as God's Word. For the Greeks '*logos*' was the rational principle in accordance with which the universe existed. It was also a useful term for describing any form of self-expression, and so the Word was also that aspect of God which is directed outward upon the world and through which creation takes place. In the Old Testament we see these ideas virtually replicated, for it is the Word of God which is the instrument of creation: God said, 'Let...'[3] and the prophetic witness uses simply 'the Word of the Lord'. So we have rationality not only as an essential element of the created order, but also as the mode of God's self-expression. This expression, and this rationality, we believe, reach their fullness in Jesus Christ.

In other words (so-to-speak, for it is here that we come to the main problem of 'God-talk', where words actually fail us), this is the point at which our humanity meets divinity. That great defender of orthodoxy, St Athanasius, didn't mince his words, 'He was man that we might be made God'![4] Theophilus of Antioch echoed this view of the '*Imago Dei*', 'God gave man an opportunity for progress so that by growing and becoming mature and furthermore having been declared a god, he might also ascend into heaven.'[5] 'Wow' (we might say)! All sorts of theological demarcation lines are being crossed here. Indeed, one Anglican theologian has actually identified the 'process' as 'a kind of transcendent anthropology...with christhood as the goal towards which created existence moves.'[6]

This is not, as some might complain, God being made in the image of man,[7] rather it is a clear determination of the implications of taking Jesus' humanity as seriously as his divinity – something seldom achieved in the history of Christian doctrine

– and so being able to work through the implications of our own human nature imaging that of God. For the writer of the *Letter to the Hebrews*, Jesus Christ was the 'spitting image' of God,[8] just as for a late Archbishop of Canterbury, 'God is Christlike and in him is no un-Christlikeness at all'.[9]

If God is to be found in Christ, not simply in his divinity, but also in his humanity, then we may indeed celebrate human rationality as a potential not to be taken lightly. For Jesus 'is not more than a man, with something extra that others haven't got, but the man in whom God perfectly comes through... he is God expressed... humanly.'[10] Neither are such insights limited to Christianity. The philosopher, Prophyry, spoke of life itself being a 'prayer to God, by inquiring into and imitating the divine nature. For inquiring purifies us, and *imitation deifies us*, by moving us nearer to God.'[11]

Not only are we made in the image of God, but it is also our human vocation so to renew that image, that humanity is, in a sense, deified! This is really what being in God's image means. Such a staggering concept consolidates possibility and rationality, and it pushes us inexorably towards responsibility – how else can we truly reflect the nature of God? – and, ultimately, because we cannot do so without God's help, to an all-embracing hope.

Responsibility

So God created man in his own image, in the image of God he created him; male and female he created them. God blessed them and said to them, 'Be fruitful and increase, fill the earth and subdue it.' (Genesis 1.27-28)

FOR DISCUSSION:

1. *Can we teach 'responsibility'?*

2. *How far does our curriculum enable pupils to feel responsibility for the earth?*

3. *Is morality a cross-curricular concern in the school?*

4. *What can Religious Education contribute to moral education?*

We are led, in valuing our being as the image of God, directly to our need to respond to this privilege with due responsibility. In curricular terms pupils need to recognize various forms of responsibility – for working collaboratively, for taking charge (at least to a certain extent) of one's own learning, and so on. We might put this another way by suggesting that even the conscience needs educating! In our Christian context the exercise of responsibility is, arguably, an even greater imperative than it is in the secular world. Why?

As with a general 'theology of education', the clue to understanding this is to be found in a robust doctrine of creation, where God has given us the responsibility of being co-creators. This may be considered with general reference to ecological issues, or with specific regard to the responsibility for bringing up (and educating!) children. A word that will ring all kinds of bells is 'stewardship'.[1] It may, again more generally, be worked through the curriculum by reference to history (which might reasonably be called 'the history of irresponsibility': human history is not often an inspiring example of what we ought to be like!), science (the need to take responsibility for our awesome 'discoveries') and so on. In general pupils need to be educated in responsibility simply because there is so much irresponsibility surrounding them in the society in which they live. The use of words like 'ought' and 'ought not' indicate that we are (at last?) embracing the moral curriculum.

All religions have a moral dimension, but religious people have no monopoly on morality. Some, looking at the history of religions – not least at Christianity with its so-called Wars of Religion, the Inquisition and so on – might even question there being a link at all! Responsibility lies at the basis of all morality. We cannot be both moral and irresponsible. There is no responsible amorality, just as there can be no responsible immorality.

Literally, 'responsibility' is about being answerable for our actions. We must 'respond' to what we choose, or choose not, to do. In a society that seems to place rather more emphasis on rights than on responsibilities, the Church school (or any school) will not have an easy task in educating for responsibility. So many people seem to be unaware of any need to 'respond' to, or be responsible for, their actions. The car driver with the blaring stereo, the smoker in a public place, or the dog walker on our school playing fields will often appeal to their 'freedom' as being the most basic issue, regardless of other entitlements to freedom such as peace outside your home, the ability to breathe fresh (or relatively fresh) air in a shop or office, or the possibility of a child playing football without falling into dog excreta (with all the consequent health risks). Intriguingly, those who champion such simple desires (peace and quiet, unpolluted grass) are then portrayed as 'fascists' for so doing! Here is the crux of any programme of moral education: just how are responsibilities and rights to be balanced?

The answer cannot simply be taught through debate, however important that is for the developing rational being (or 'becoming'?). While, presumably, it is possible to teach the difference between right and wrong as an academic exercise, it is another thing entirely for the child to grasp the concept through will and emotion. We mentioned the conscience above. Whatever else that might be, it certainly involves some kind of self-understanding: how we measure up to our ideals and our potentialities. Only when the whole person so engages him/herself in the search for responsibility can s/he truly have the capacity to answer for his/her actions. Recognizing what the conscience is telling us is one thing: doing something about it is quite another. All our human faculties need to be engaged by the moral curriculum. As we have already seen, understanding 'ought' and 'ought not' is not just the outcome of being told. Research has shown that, as in many other areas of human development, our moral capacities develop only gradually, and at different speeds, passing through various stages (e.g. conformity – behaving as expected; expediency – behaving because it is convenient for us to do so) before being completely internalized as a system of moral values. Perhaps some people never achieve this internalization? The curriculum of a Church school should address these issues directly. If we simply assume that moral values are implicit in what we teach, we may, to our eventual horror, find they were never there at all. This is where some form of explicit moral education, perhaps via Personal and Social Education (PSE), might be helpful.

Hope

> If it is for this life only that Christ has given us hope, we of all men are most to be pitied. (1 Corinthians 15.19)

FOR DISCUSSION:

1. *How can we most effectively bring hope where there is despair?*

2. *Do the stories we tell pupils have vision and hope?*

3. *Can we teach a realistic hope?*

4. *How well do we handle issues of death and bereavement?*

5. *Are we able to show, in the curriculum, where a message of hope is available to our pupils?*

We may often feel that we live in a world or a society in which all hope has been lost (existentialists might stamp the words at the gate of hell[1] on every foetus!); it may be that schools are working with literally 'hopeless' families, and sometimes there may be an understandable tendency to reflect that hopelessness. It is equally clear that there are some secular schools which do indeed bring hope 'where there is despair'.[2] But again, hope, is a Christian imperative, and so a value essential (not just 'good') in our Church schools.

Moreover, the hope of the world is often plain 'optimism' – 'it'll be OK in the end'. The humanistic doctrine of progress tells us that humanity is 'improving' all the time. In so doing it not only devalues the past, but it also leads us in all kinds of spheres of life to assume that 'we moderns know best'! 'The past is a foreign country; they do things differently there.'[3] Indeed; but doesn't travel broaden the mind? Of course, rather some optimism at least than a despairing pessimism. There can be little doubt that one of the reasons why modern science-fiction myths are so popular, is that they sometimes show a future where, on the whole, we have managed to find peace and justice, and where starvation is a thing of the past. They are also wonder-full, 'Star Trek is a marvellous journey and its appeal derives from the traditional devices of the vision, the dream, the legend and the wonder.'[4]

Nevertheless, we have to ask the question: however beguiling, is such optimism based on any kind of realistic assessment of life? Secular optimism may be fairly shallow, however appealing it may seem in a world which needs so much hope. There is also, of course, what we might term a religious optimism which is just as beguiling, and just as dangerous, as its secular counterpart. This is the notion, particularly prevalent in Islam, but also to be found in fundamentalist Christianity, that whatever happens, it will all be for the best in the end. God has it all under control. Such determinism is not only, as we have argued above, theologically dubious in its arrogance and complacency; but it is also quite literally hope-less and unhelpful in the traumas of everyday living. Try telling the parent whose child is dying of cancer that it will be 'all right in the end'! As the Doctrine Commission's report *The Mystery of Salvation* points out quite starkly, 'Death remains a deep challenge to belief in a God of love.'[5] We have already seen that we must not trivialize the mystery.

True Christian hope will, therefore, not be tidy; but should be full-blooded, for it takes full account of the evil and suffering that there is in the world. The point of Christian hope, which ought to be founded on humility in the face of the mystery of suffering, is that it is there to transform, not simply accept. As such it is, like love, immensely vulnerable. In that vulnerability, it may appear weak; but that weakness is merely the engagement of reality with compassion. In this sense, such hope is not a triumphant hope, it is more like a sensitive flower. We need to teach our children to recognize and to value it. Ironically, the world which places such store on optimism is so full of 'angst' (what percentage of Americans have psychiatric help?) that Christian hope becomes a real life-enhancing weapon, one which should be in the armoury of every child. But, again, it doesn't grow on trees: hope needs teaching, it needs a basis that pure secularism just cannot provide, and it needs to be experienced. There are many children in danger of being overwhelmed by hopelessness. Our Church schools, part of a hope-based organization, may be well placed to give hope real value and real meaning.

Risk

> And in the middle of the garden he set the tree of life and the tree of the knowledge of good and evil. (Genesis 2.9)

FOR DISCUSSION:

1. *What risks might occur in the life of one of our pupils?*

2. *Identify some positive and necessary risks to which pupils should be exposed.*

3. *Can the Religious Education teacher, with integrity, commend the 'risk of faith'?*

4. *Do you think that we (teachers, parents and children) are, in any sense, co-creators with God?*

Life is a risky business, and that risk is both invaluable and essential. Sometimes our society does all it can to avoid or even eliminate risk. There may be good reasons for this since *risk assessment* is high on the agenda of every school. That, however, is a forlorn hope – risk *is* part of the universe: we might even say that it is part of the ambiguity of the universe. It has been pointed out time and again by those, such as John Hick in his book *Evil and the God of Love*, who are seeking to produce a viable theodicy that risk is an essential part of the forming of a human person.[1] Without risk we would be nothing – mere 'pets', pampered and protected by a God who wraps us in cotton wool.

There will always be some who would prefer this scenario, but it is not our human vocation. In mythical terms, the mere placing of the tree in the Garden of Eden is representative of the tremendous risk taken by the Creator God. Of course, God might not have taken the risk; but not to take risk is tantamount to doing *nothing*

– and the One-who-loves can never do nothing. 'There is no question of God's not creating... for him to be super-generous is just for him to be himself. He creates because, being God, he gives.'[2] As co-creative parents and teachers we share the risk that all we seek to provide our children (I refer now specifically to moral and spiritual teaching) may be thrown back in our face; or, to change the metaphor appropriately, nailed to a cross.

We need, therefore, to enable our children to value risk. They should not take silly risks with their lives (like playing 'chicken' which is unnecessary and meaningless). However, they need to value the way that risk enables us to develop as people, to be courageous and adventurous while, at the same time, being caring and helpful towards those who take risks on our behalf. In particular we would point to those who take either the risk of faith, (which will be discussed later) or the risk of *unfaith* (which is not the same as no faith for the atheistic position is equally faithful). In so doing we take seriously St Paul's reminder that we do not yet see 'face to face' because our spiritual vision is restricted to seeing 'in a mirror dimly'. (1 Corinthians 13.12)

The fundamental risk is, of course, that of being wrong and so the most ultimate risk is being ultimately wrong – or wrong about ultimate things. Why?

> To be finite is to live in risk and uncertainty, and... we have to commit ourselves to policies of action without complete knowledge of all the relevant circumstances and... consequences that will flow from the action. Our life in this world is not one that can be based only upon the certitude of knowledge – the man who tries to live this way, without risk, never really lives at all – but one that must go out in faith.[3]

The Christian teacher does his pupils no favours by refusing to face the reality and depth of our ignorance – at the appropriate

age and time, of course – and the importance for our development of accepting that. It is at this point that we are driven back
(or better – forward) to hope:

> In this present life good can often not in fact be brought
> out of evil. Life's pains and agonies, which sometimes help
> to create stronger and more compassionate men and
> women, at other times overwhelm and crush, leaving only
> despair, tragedy and disintegration. It is at this point that
> the myth [of theodicy] speaks of continuation of the
> creative process beyond this life and of its ultimate success
> in a limitless good which will justify everything that has
> formed the contingent series of events leading to it.
> Experiencing life's baffling mixture of good and evil in
> terms of this myth, we may be helped to live in hope,
> trusting in the ultimate sovereignty of God's love.[4]

In our Church schools we must take responsibility for proper
risk-education. Yes – this will be about ensuring that our children
take no unnecessary physical risks, but it will also mean affirming
the centrality of risk in our personal formation. This may seem,
on the surface at least, somewhat bleak. But it isn't. Because it is
only in the midst of ambiguity that a real faith is possible. Indeed,
it is precisely this faith that provides stability and unification in
our personal lives and in our relationships. This is central, not
least because it was this risk which God took in the incarnation.
It is the risk we share all the time simply by being parents and
teachers.

Christian values within the school community

A sacramental universe

> When the Lord saw that Moses had turned aside to look [at the burning bush], he called to him out of the bush, 'Moses, Moses.' And Moses answered, 'Yes, I am here.' (Exodus 3.4-5)

FOR DISCUSSION:

1. *How can we enable pupils to find God in the midst of everyday life?*

2. *Can and should Church schools be sacramental communities?*

3. *How can we best enable our pupils to understand how the value of certain things may change?*

4. *Are there any problems in celebrating the Eucharist in the school? Are these problems capable of resolution?*

What exactly did catch Moses' eye? What is something extraordinary? A real bush that burned supernaturally? Or was it a natural phenomenon of some kind that enabled Moses to perceive the Beyond in its depths? A strong theology of the sacramental makes 'the things of this world so transparent that in them and through them we know God's presence and activity in our very midst, and we experience his grace.'[1]

We live in one world which has two aspects: these aspects are often reflected in dichotomies – material/spiritual, secular/sacred, ordinary/extraordinary, natural/supernatural. Human beings themselves may be viewed in the same way as a psycho-somatic (mind–body) unity. This dichotomy often causes tensions; for many people the problem is in coming to terms with those tensions, 'That nature sets its desires against the Spirit, while the Spirit fights against it. They are in conflict with one another so that what you will to do you cannot do.'[2] Problems occur when one-sided solutions are sought, so the Christian community will be one in which the 'both-and' are valued, where there is such balance that children perceive that unity which enables them to value the world (whichever world – that of the school, the home, the local community) as one in which God may be experienced.

This requires us to develop school communities which are both implicitly and explicitly sacramental. Implicitly the Church school ought to mediate the grace of God in its very life. Explicitly, it is likely that at least one of the recognized Christian sacraments – the Eucharist – will have a central role in the worshipping life of the school. As some theologians move away from the concept of transubstantiation as a way of seeking to interpret and to understand the Eucharistic Presence, simply because the philosophical ideas on which it is based are no longer as helpful as they were, one of the new ways of thinking about it is actually known as 'transvaluation'. Here we may understand that, as the eucharistic elements are consecrated, they become the body and blood of Christ:

> simply through their becoming effectual symbols, but wherever the significance of an effectual symbol is certain and considerable, we naturally think of it in terms of its natural properties. We do not carefully separate in thought the natural properties of a florin and its purchasing value; rather we combine the two, and we think of the

florin quite simply as an object which has certain natural properties and certain purchasing value. We tend to think of the latter as to all intents and purposes a property of the object; yet it depends simply and solely on the fact that the object is an effectual symbol.[3]

So with the bread and wine. We take these very simple things, and God changes their value out of all recognition. From being mere things of the Earth, they become elements *sub specie aeternitatis*. Here, therefore, a philosophy of value is actually to be found at the heart of the Christian sacraments. This, if nothing else, should inspire us to take very seriously indeed, the place of 'values' in our Church schools, for the sacraments are essentially 'valuable'.

Signs and symbols of transcendence

In the year of King Uzziah's death I saw the Lord seated on a throne, high and exalted, and skirt of his robe filled the temple. Above him were attendant seraphim. (Isaiah 6.1-2)

FOR DISCUSSION:

1. *What symbols, both explicit and implicit, are to be found in the school?*

2. *Which symbols are past their 'sell-by date', and what new symbols may be meaningful to our pupils?*

3. *Are there any secular symbols which can re-interpret the sacred?*

4. *How might we improve the use of music in worship?*

5. *Can we pray without words?*

The impact of the transcendent on our finite lives has been discussed with specific reference to the curriculum. Isaiah's vision was probably centred in the worship of the Temple: the antiphonal singing, the smoke of the incense permeating the sanctuary. All these things of the world signalled the transcendent in the midst. It is sad that this kind of sublimity has been lost in many of our churches. Is it even less likely to be found in schools? Possibly so, for our British empiricist legacy has tended to dominate the secular curriculum, and many agreed syllabuses for RE have found shelter in the purely phenomenological: 'Just describe it; for heaven's sake don't engage with it' has often been the message. But that should not be good enough for our Church schools:

> Symbolism cannot live with literalism. Yet it can also be claimed that humans, without symbolism, cannot truly live. If a symbol is to retain its vitality it must be constantly re-adapted and re-interpreted within fresh contexts.[1]

Here is a great opportunity for Church schools which, through specific rituals, experiences and traditions, can provide eye-opening (and ear-opening) experiences for children which they may find lacking elsewhere in their lives. In school, probably more than in Church, there will be the chance to experiment and explore new ways of enriching old symbols, so that they can speak again to a new generation. The school community will point towards, and provide means for pupils to apprehend, the Other. Some of these means will be through the use of explicit and recognizable Christian symbols, such as the cross or icons. Others may be more implicit.

Of course, they will not all be visual. As I write this paragraph I am listening to Allegri's 'Miserere mei, Deus'. This piece of music has always, for me, had that elusive 'tingle factor', not least as the treble aims for, and hits, the high C! But not the music only; also the words, 'Have mercy upon me, O God, after thy great goodness. Turn thy face from my sins; and put out all my misdeeds. Make me a clean heart, O God.'[2]

All these signals combine to enable the sensitive soul to touch the ineffable. All children deserve such life-enhancing experiences. Obviously, by the very nature of such experiences, they cannot be made to order. But, who knows what we might present in school to touch an individual soul, and so remain with that child for the rest of his/her life. Whatever symbols we use, they should be chosen so as to enable the members of our community to reflect on, and in their lives be helped to reflect, ultimate Value.

Relationship

> For the Lord was passing by: a great and strong wind came rending mountains and shattering rocks before him, but the Lord was not in the wind; and after the wind there was an earthquake, but the Lord was not in the earthquake; and after the earthquake fire, but the Lord was not in the fire; and after the fire a low murmuring sound. (1 Kings 19.11-13)

FOR DISCUSSION:

1. *How can we enable our pupils to become more aware of the Other and the others in their lives?*

2. *How should school worship contribute towards this understanding?*

3. *What do we understand by, and how seriously do we treat, social education?*

We may understand that whatever Elijah experienced on the mountain or Moses at the burning bush, they had a revelation of One who was the Other – the upper cases are used deliberately to connote that the Other was indeed 'wholly Other' to them (and so to us). But there are also many 'others'. Our school communities should be able to help our children discern the way the Other and the others impact on our lives.

It was the Jewish writer, Martin Buber who, in his classic work, *I and Thou*[1], reflected on Feuerbach's dictum, 'Where there is no "thou" there is no "I".'[2] There are, of course, two dimensions: the objective in which 'I' relate to 'it', and the subjective in which 'I' relate to you ('thou'). One of the greatest lessons that we learn as human beings is that there is more to life than 'me'! This will, of course, resonate with the value of 'humility' discussed above. *Pace* Margaret Thatcher, the individual can only properly exist within society. It may be that for some this lesson is never fully absorbed. It is in the normal intercourse of life that we come to understand that we can only truly be 'I' in community (the 'thous') – this is a special value and insight of the Christian faith. It almost goes without saying that 'I' can only know 'you' insofar as you make yourself known, or allow yourself to be known, to me. And vice versa, of course.

Within the Judaeo-Christian tradition there is also a liturgical dimension 'where each and every one is "I" and all are "I" together'.[3] It is pre-eminently through public worship (in our Christian tradition, through the Eucharist) that there is much much more – the spiritual discovery of the 'Other Thou' which ultimately complements all our 'I's, and with which our 'I' is in communion. Our distinctive Christian insight, constantly affirmed in worship, is that this wholly Other Thou 'though transcendent and incomprehensible, chose, as it were, to get the divine hands dirty, and get involved in the messy business of human everyday life.'[4]

There will be a variety of loci in which these insights may be encouraged and developed – family, friendship groups, and Church; but school is a vital one.

Faith

> The Lord said to Abram, 'Leave your own country, your kinsmen, and your father's house, and go to a country that I will show you'. (Genesis 12.1)

> This is where the fortitude of God's people has its place – in keeping God's commands and remaining loyal to Jesus. (Revelation 14.12)

FOR DISCUSSION:

1. *Is it possible to commend faith without indoctrination?*

2. *Think of three ways in which the school can be a beacon of faith in the community.*

3. *How are Church schools to be distinctive?*

Our Church schools should be communities of faith. Having taken the 'risk of faith' ourselves, we are in the best position to commend the value of faith to children. But this 'commendation' is not to be confused with curricular RE, which is why I have located it in the community rather than in the curriculum. I want to affirm again my conviction that there are no grounds for curricular RE, even in a Church school, being a vehicle for evangelism. To do so is to betray the educational cause in which we are seeking to 'lead out' the child into autonomous person-hood; it is not for us in our schools to tell him/her what to think and believe. Nevertheless, 'faith' must be one of the central values for a Church school, which will not be shared by secular schools.

It is, therefore, the locus of a central dichotomy between educa-tion and nurture (not to be confused with confessional RE) with which our schools ought to be concerned. On the one hand, for the sake of the integrity of our educational task we are not to indoctrinate; on the other, 'We have a Gospel to proclaim!' (Eddie Burn's wonderful hymn[1]). This is where it is necessary to be clear about the nature of 'faith' as a Christian value. For many people 'faith' is simply a matter of belief, and so orthodoxy (as opposed to heresy) is literally about believing the right things. Again, for many (it often appears) who might be said to subscribe to the 'Wonderland' school of theology, it doesn't matter how odd our beliefs are. In fact, sometimes, the odder the better, because to believe such things must mean we have great faith. And if we find such belief difficult, all we need to do is keep at it and, like the White Queen, draw a long breath, shut our eyes, and practise. 'When I was your age, I always did it for half-an-hour a day. Why, sometimes I've believed as many as six impossible things before breakfast.'[2] But faith such as this is narrow and, ultimately, sterile. Faith must embrace every aspect of our lives. As such it is probably better to imagine faith as an attitude to life. It will imply the holding of certain beliefs, even the *apophatic 'via negativa'* (i.e. the belief that we can really know nothing about God), but it will not be limited to matters of belief. Indeed, the faith-full (faithful) ought to be so secure in their faith, that they can confi-dently and productively disagree on matters of belief (mistakenly called 'matters of faith').

The openness which is implicit in a wider view of faith will, there-fore, mean that the person of faith will not be afraid to put his faith to the test. Such faith will be more than just cognitive; it will be like every value, attitudinal as well, that is, both affective (pertaining to the emotions) and conative (related to volition, desire and the will). It will recognize that we cannot know all there is to know, that, indeed, we may be wrong more than occasionally. Again, this is not some cerebral or academic kind of acknowledgement; it is an intrinsic recognition of the contingent[3] nature of our being, and what that means for our lives. In recognizing the ambiguity of human existence, it will inevitably have the aspect of a leap in the dark. That notion is well in keeping with our emphasis on the positive value of risk. It will also carry an important element of trust. You do not leap in the dark unless you have some notion that there will be someone, or even something, there to catch you!

It is here that the two biblical quotations (above) may be seen to point to two important aspects of faith. As the Letter of James reminds us, Abraham went out in faith.

> Coming almost immediately after the story of the Tower of Babel, which presents a dark picture of human pride and ambition, the story of the call of Abraham is like a burst of light that illuminates the whole landscape.[4]

The history of the Patriarchs is that of a pilgrim movement towards a goal set by God. In purely human terms what they did was 'plain daft'; and yet this was their response to the impinging of the Divine on their lives. Whatever the exact nature of that awareness, it was not simply a result of studying comparative religion! It was something which involved 'the whole person'; something which touched them to the core. The result was response and commitment. That is the first step. Having taken that step, faith requires considerable perseverance (which could be another value); staying with it, having 'fortitude' and 'loyalty'. In other words: keeping the faith.

Neither is the leap in the dark completely blind. There are various lights, if we only know how to look for them, and how to use them. Both the individual and the community of faith have a duty to work hard on clarifying the essentials of the Faith. It is here that the role of the school as a community of faith becomes important, and can operate in such a way as not to compromise its main, educational, responsibility. If we have ensured that matters of belief are properly contextualized as an aspect of faith and, in so doing, have made it clear (in line with our emphasis on truth and rationality) that matters of belief may be (at least to a certain extent) negotiable, in the sense that they are not the be all and end all of faith, then we shall be able, in good faith (!), to act more like guides, or even lights, in order that our children may journey safely. Essential for this, and probably prior to it, is the need for the community of faith to actively commend the journey. There are, regrettably, many parents who would encourage their children, at least by example, not to bother. The Church school will, by its life and work, commend the option of a life of faith, as literally the only life worth living. In this, it may often find itself in conflict with the values of the world: another reason why Church schools are called to be distinctive.

Commitment

> [Jesus began to pray] 'Father, if it be thy will, take this cup away from me. Yet not my will but thine be done.' (Luke 22.42)

FOR DISCUSSION:

1. *What are the signs of commitment in the school?*

2. *In a multi-faith Church school, can pupils and staff worship together without compromising either their faith, or the faith of others?*

3. *'Multi-faith Religious Education is particularly essential in a Church school that has only Christian children.' Do you agree?*

4. *How can the school maintain a Christian ethos when over 90 per cent of the children are Muslim?*

Commitment is a universal value and, as such, is not confined to Church schools. But it may be considered that, as communities of faithful people, our Church schools will exemplify this value more than any other institution. After all, as we have seen, commitment is an essential aspect of faith. The story of Jesus in Gethsemane is a tremendous example of commitment. Even when the cost is ultimate, he stays on the road to Calvary. Of course, commitment does require a vision for the future. We need to strive to see the whole picture, insofar as we are able to do so.

Without commitment we are without direction, and we will simply move through our lives in the control of events. Commitment implies a determination to do what we can to take control of our lives. This value is one learned more by example than by anything else. If the school is not obviously committed to its task, then pupils will take note, just as they note when their parents drop them off at church, and then go home again.

There is another aspect of commitment which is a particular issue for our multi-faith Church schools. How possible is it to be committed to our own faith and, at the same time, be open to the faith of others? There can be no doubt of our vocation to 'stand up for Jesus'! Nevertheless, over many years there has been a clear process of coming to terms with the existence, and then the existence in our midst, of faiths other than our own. This has often been quite grudging on both sides. The Roman Catholic Church, however, made a positive affirmation at Vatican II, 'Other religions to be found everywhere strive variously to answer the restless searchings of the human heart...[therefore] the Catholic Church rejects nothing which is true and holy in these religions.'[1]

While other Christians have been less enthusiastic – believing indeed, that other faiths are simply in error – there has generally been a growing recognition that the Copernican revolution in astronomy must be succeeded by a similar change of perspective in theology:

It involves a shift from the dogma that Christianity is at the centre to the realisation that it is God who is at the centre and that all the religions of mankind, including our own, serve and revolve around Him.[2]

To make this kind of assertion, however, even if all were to be in agreement with it, does not solve the dichotomy of openness and commitment. Is it possible to be committed to my own faith while being open to the possibility that God may be met by others through theirs? There can be no doubt of the practical importance of this, especially for those Church schools serving other faith communities. Here, very often, the Christian may feel that the explicit faithfulness of those they meet will allow no other kind of response than that of John Hick in multi-faith Birmingham:

I have myself encountered men and women who are manifestly much closer to God, and living much more fully in response to God, than most of us, and whose very existence challenges our traditional exclusivist theories. For they are people to whom God is the supreme reality, and they walk humbly before him, their lives revealing the presence of God's spirit within them.[3]

Nevertheless, if we reject the so-called 'exclusivist' view of Christianity's relationship with other faiths, we should also be careful not to fall into the trap, signposted above in our discussion of humility, of a relativism in which all are really the same. On occasions one has to wonder whether Hick might not have fallen into this trap himself:

It is not appropriate to speak of a religion as being true or false, any more than it is to speak of a civilisation being true or false... the same differences between the eastern and western minds, expressed in different conceptual and linguistic, social, political and artistic forms, presumably underlie the contrasts between eastern and western forms of religion.[4]

To be committed is to value that to which we are committed; and, as we have argued above, an essential value is truth. Therefore, issues of truth and falsity, the possibility of perversions and distortions within religious faiths, must all be taken seriously. We must, for example, always be open to the possibility that we may learn new truths, and that these truths may be found in other traditions. We should certainly guard against pronouncing on traditions of which we have no experience. We have seen that a part of the risk of life is our relative ignorance. It is inevitable that our perspectives are limited. We do not have a God's-eye-view!

The way forward must be, at least in part, embracing the value of humility and recognizing ourselves for what we are: limited beings. We do not know everything; we are people of our culture and of our time; our lives are relatively short, and our universe is vast. Who knows what secrets lie out there?

> Nor, in our little day,
> May his devices with the heavens be guessed,
> His pilgrimage to thread the Milky Way
> Or his bestowals there be manifest.
>
> But in the eternities,
> Doubtless we shall compare together, hear
> A million alien Gospels, in what guise
> He trod the Pleiades, the Lyre, the Bear.
> O, be prepared my soul!
> To read the inconceivable, to scan
> The million forms of God those stars unroll
> When, in our turn, we show to them a Man.[5]

Once again we are lost in awe and wonder. How dare we act as though we have it all tied up? Is it not an essential value to be so committed to God that we want to rejoice in our faith with other people of faith, even though our faiths are different? Indeed, as we look at a world in which faith so often seems to be in short supply, we recognize that people of faith should stand together. That is not to recommend syncretism; that would be quite wrong, for it threatens the integrity of all faiths. But syncretism really has no need to be an issue, provided that we are clear as to where we stand – and careful where we tread!

> A Christian committed to his faith may take that faith as definitive and believe that in Christ is the fullness of truth. But he would have to say that neither he as an individual nor the Christian Church in its corporate life has ever fully comprehended this truth. He would, therefore, be open to learn more of the truth of Christ, even to deepen his Christian commitment, through his contacts with non-Christian religions, or even secular ideologies.[6]

Within our Christian school communities we should be proud to share our insights with children of other faiths, in such a way as not to threaten their integrity, or question our commitment. Once again, this will not be easy. All sorts of issues must be considered and resolved about worship, and about a host of other, probably more cultural, matters that could cause concern (e.g. mixed PE). Provided we hold fast to essential values, our journey should not only be very interesting, but it should also be truly enlightening.[7]

Acceptance

> In Christ he chose us before the world was founded, to be dedicated, to be without blemish in his sight, to be full of love; and he destined us... to be accepted as his sons through Jesus Christ. (Ephesians 1.4-5)

FOR DISCUSSION:

1. *Do staff, governors, parents and pupils find the school an accepting community?*

2. *What are the implications of the above for staff and pupil discipline?*

3. *Does the Church school have any role in supporting, or even being a surrogate for, those parents who find it difficult to take, or who are not interested in taking the baptismal commitments seriously?*

This is the other side of the commitment 'coin'. It would appear that a central truth about the human condition is our dissatisfaction with it. That is not in itself a bad thing, because it is right to be dissatisfied with imperfection. However, this dissatisfaction sometimes runs so deep within our personal and social lives that it becomes like a cancer eating away at our selfhood – we are, and never will be satisfied. Whatever we have, we want more. But the more is most often that which may well be expensive, but have no real value: bigger house, bigger car, better holidays. None of these things have anything to do with us as human beings. In order to protect our sense of worth, without which we can never become whole, and to drive our sense of commitment, we need to learn how to accept what we are (I do not mean this to connote a 'do nothing – everything is as ordained by God' attitude, exemplified by 'the rich man in his castle, the poor man at his gate',[1] i.e. just put up with it!). If things are wrong, they need changing. But lacking perfection is a given of life, and it is that given which, if we do not accept it, means we will never value ourselves for what we are: children of God.

This is the tremendous insight of St Paul, to be rediscovered in liberating surprise and joy by Martin Luther: God has accepted us for what we are, 'warts and all',[2] and we have joined the divine 'family'. As in every family, each of us has different talents and different perspectives. In our Christian communities we need to enable our children to value themselves as they are. Yes, if (as there will be) there are ways we can improve ourselves (in every sense) then we shouldn't be frightened to do so. Schools can play an important role in enabling all our children, whatever their ability, size, and colour to accept their God-given life, and so make something of it. But a part of the current malaise is to be so dissatisfied with what we are, so guilt-ridden (and religion hasn't helped), that we cannot accept ourselves. If we cannot accept ourselves, we will not be able to accept others.

These are twin prongs: we need to accept ourselves, because God has accepted us 'as sons'; so must we accept others because they have already been accepted by God. Who are we to question God's judgement? As we have seen, however, this is not an excuse to forget that there is still work to be done by us so that we can 'grow in the grace and knowledge... of Christ'.[3] In other words our 'justification' (to use the central term of the Reformation) is not simply something extrinsic to us, it is also integral to our Christian lives.

It is here that the Christian community, especially that represented by the Church of England – as a part of which we work in our schools – is in not a little disarray. It is inappropriate here to consider all the issues related to infant baptism, but in reflecting on our role as an accepting community we do need to consider how we might provide at least part of the community context in which we realize (in the sense of 'make real') the welcome which we offer at the end of each baptism:

> We welcome you into the Lord's family.
> We are members together of the body of Christ;
> We are children of the same heavenly Father;
> We are inheritors together of the kingdom of God.[4]

It would appear to be increasingly the case that the majority of children baptized are not given 'the help and encouragement' of their biological family 'to be faithful in public worship and private prayer, to live and trust in God...', despite promises made.[5] So it will inevitably fall to the Church, most often in the form of the Church school (for our Church schools will interact with far more children than our individual churches) to provide it. After all, we are 'members together... children of the same heavenly Father... inheritors together...'

Unless Christian baptism is understood so completely to be an act *ex opere operato*, that it matters not what happens afterwards (and so we degenerate towards an almost magical view of the sacraments), it presumably makes some difference as to whether the Holy Baptism elicits any ultimate response from the baptized. To return to our acceptance by God:

> The principle danger is that justification gets separated from actual growth in righteousness or in the Christian virtues...[and] thought of as something external, a so-called 'forensic' justification, a kind of acquittal... that takes no account of the condition of the person so acquitted.[6]

While this is a gracious act of God which we neither deserve nor earn, it is difficult to imagine that is all there is to it (however great, wonderful, etc. the 'all' is). At this point we need to fall back on analogy which, by definition, does not provide an exact comparison, but hopefully will provide enough ideas to give us a flavour of what we are talking about. Might we not consider that baptism without genuine commitment (vicarious or otherwise) is like receiving our driving licence (which we all treasure, and which we were all ecstatic to finally obtain!) and then never driving a car again? A number of points may be made: what's the purpose of having a licence? Is it not true that most of us really learn to drive after we have received our licence? (You can see that I am trying to avoid importing the notion of passing a test – although there was an important element of that in Early Christian baptism.) Ultimately, of course, (due to infirmity), the licence may be withdrawn. Here the analogy breaks down.

Or does it? Let us not put *that* to the test! If our acceptance by God is to take place on any personal level, then it must surely involve at least some kind of free acceptance and co-operation on our part? This is not to imply that the divine action depends on that; we must always protect God's initiative in all things. But unless we are involved somehow in our redemption, then there will always be a sense in which it is irrelevant to us and to our lives. It will be just another 'thing' which happens to us whether we like it or not.

In other words, not only must we accept ourselves because God has accepted us, but we must also, at least to a certain extent, accept God's acceptance. Children will not do that in a vacuum. If the drawing out of the potentiality that our baptism offers is not nurtured within the biological family, then it may be – it must be – within the Christian family of the school. The initiative is still God's; the Church school is his instrument. The gift has been given, but it demands to be accepted. We know, indeed, that our own commitment, which is our response to the grace we have accepted, needs to be constantly renewed – that is one of the reasons why we have liturgical opportunities to renew our own baptismal vows. This renewal will, hopefully, be accompanied by a deepening in our understanding of the nature of our faith response, and so a deepening of our commitment to it. There will be those occasions when faith breaks down under some intolerable strain, and it is at that point that we ourselves need the 'help and encouragement' – and the unconditional acceptance – of our fellow members of the Body of Christ.

Grace

> You must work out your own salvation in fear and trembling; for it is God who works in you, inspiring both the will and the deed, for his own chosen purpose. (Philippians 2.12-13)

FOR DISCUSSION:

1. *In what ways could our school be described as a 'channel of God's grace'?*

2. *Is our community thankful enough?*

3. *What are the signs of a Spirit-filled school community?*

Into our sacramental universe comes the gift of God. In a narrow sense we may understand that this 'amazing grace' is mediated by the sacraments. The broader interpretation (above) invites us to be sacramental communities, not just in the sense that we administer sacraments (although we may do that), but communities in which God's grace (which, as St Thomas remarked 'does not abolish nature but perfects it',[1]) can firstly be recognized, and then received.

Within Christian theology there has always been at least some recognition of what Donald Baillie termed 'the paradox of grace', reflecting St Paul's cry of faith 'yet not I but the grace of God within me'.[2] It is our particular conviction:

> which a Christian man possesses, that every good thing in him, every good thing he does, is somehow not wrought

by himself but by God. This is a highly paradoxical conviction, for in ascribing all to God it does not abrogate
human personality nor disclaim personal responsibility.
Never is human action more truly and fully personal,
never does the agent feel more perfectly free, than in those
moments of which he can say as a Christian that whatever
good was in them was not his but God's.'[3]

God's gift goes hand in hand with our decision to accept the life
of faith. In so doing we seek to conform ourselves to Jesus Christ,
whose own decision was to be obedient to the Father. In offering
his life and his will to God, the divine grace operated pre-
eminently through him. And – here is the nub of the paradox – it
was that very obedience that gave freedom. To want to save our
lives is to lose them; yet to lose ourselves in the life of God is
salvation.[4] In God's service is perfect freedom! This paradox
simply emphasizes the mysterious character of grace which:

> is bestowed in the essence of the soul and is received into
> her powers; for if the soul is to effect anything... she must
> needs have grace by virtue of which to transcend her own
> activities such as knowing and loving.[5]

Such is, of course, nothing other than the work of the Holy Spirit.
While it may seem trite to say that our school communities should
work to become communities of the Spirit, this is, nevertheless, an
essential feature of our vocation as Christians in education. That
is why, for example, our governors' meetings should call upon
God, the Holy Spirit, in prayer before they attempt to deal with
the burdens, and it so often is a burden, of the day. Here we are
distinctive. Prayer has all but disappeared from secular life (how
much longer will Parliament find it necessary to 'call on the
Lord'?). Governing bodies of County schools have nothing upon
which to rely but their Articles – and those for not much longer![6]
Within a community in which prayer is seen to be important, such
an explicit conviction that God's grace is, indeed, available to us

in our work, should percolate down to the awareness of pupils. These are the resources by which we can begin to contend with life!

Judgement

> Lord, when was it that we saw you hungry or thirsty or a stranger or naked or ill or in prison, and did nothing for you? (Matthew 25.44)

FOR DISCUSSION:

1. *How can we best enable our pupils to realize their potential?*

2. *Is our community judgemental?*

3. *How do we deal with competition: corporate and personal?*

4. *How can we best value the judgements of inspection?*

Judgement is not the antithesis of grace! It is its other aspect. It is when we are faced with grace that we find ourselves at one and the same time judged. Communities which point to grace, must at the same time point to judgement. You can't have one without the other! But surely judgement is not something to be feared. It is something to be valued. In a relatively trivial manner, pupils will be judged academically. That judgement can, indeed, become demonic as both children and their schools come under the pressure of escalating competition (I [We] cannot value myself as myself; I [We] can only value myself as judged against the others). Just as our Christian schools must encourage and enable self-acceptance, so must they facilitate self-judgement. Again, at a basic level, it is not my academic achievement measured against others that is most significant, it is the measurement of that achievement against my ability.

However, we must strive to operate within our communities at a much more profound level. It is, after all, God's judgement which exposes each of us as we really are. While our role is not to sit in judgement ourselves, we do our children a disservice if we do not enable them to value in their lives the claims of God upon them. Merely to think eschatologically is missing the point. Whatever will happen *post-mortem* is best left to God! We need to examine realistically the meaning of the value of judgement for our lives now, and that is often problematic due to the traditional emphasis of the tradition on future judgement. It was also a problem for St John, which is why the Fourth Gospel affirms that the believer already 'has eternal life', and has already 'passed from death to life'; even that 'the judgement of this world' is now.[1] Known as 'realized eschatology', the Johannine solution is appealing.

The Greek '*krisis*' – 'judgement' – sets the tone well! For John the 'crisis' is needing to respond to the call of Jesus. Those who believe in him may be acquitted and saved; those who reject him are to be condemned. And yet: 'it was not to judge the world that God sent his Son into the world; but that through him the world might be saved'.[2] The apparent paradox is considered by C.K. Barrett:

> The process of judgement is an inseparable concomitant of salvation; no real contradiction is involved when Jesus says that he came both not to judge, and to judge... [And, quoting Bultmann] 'To be judged is simply to shut our hearts to grace' is nearly but not quite adequate. [But, as Bultmann also says] 'In the decision man makes when faced with the question put to him by God, it becomes apparent, in his very act of decision, what he really is.'[3]

'Who am I?' is both the natural human cry (not often articulated as directly as this) and our abiding dilemma. It is certainly the driving force of our 'growing up', as we seek to discover ourselves in a world of others. 'How am I different?' Perhaps, more poignantly: 'Why am I so different?' – leading to the desire to be the same, to copy the behaviour of those we admire, but who may not be admirable! Of course, children will learn by their mistakes; that is what growing-up is all about, but the Church school community will not be shy in helping them in their search. But, 'it is not enough to help him find himself; he must find his way to a best self which will emerge only after growth and struggle.'[4]

We must beware of introspection, and of complacency. The parable of the sheep and the goats reminds us that judgement is not a cosy experience. We face hard questions throughout our lives, some asked by others, the worst asked by ourselves, and these penetrate to the very depths of our selves. Did we learn to care? At the risk of sounding trivial (simply because it is about much more than this), we may point to the efforts of our schools to focus on the needs of others. Charitable activities make an important contribution to pupils' recognition that the world is not entirely OK, and that there are things we and they need to do about it. These activities also remind us, again, that we are nothing without others. Indeed, any half-decent theology of judgement, realized or ultimate, will have a perspective that enables us to see that although we may be bothered (and it is quite natural to be so) about our individual destinies, we should not forget the bigger picture:

> The question of man's final destiny is, of course, a part of the whole question of human existence. As against this narrow concern with individual destiny... [there is] a wider concern... [which] may have in view nothing less than the whole cosmos.[5]

While, here, we are inevitably returned to hope, it is only by helping children to recognize, not only what they are, but also what they have the potential to be, as members of the school community, as members of their families, as people on their way in God's world, or even as part of the cosmic plan, that they will be able to accept the value of judgement as something infinitely to be treasured.

Forgiveness

> But while he was still a long way off his father saw him, and his heart went out to him. He ran to meet him, flung his arms round him, and kissed him. (Luke 15.20)

The motive and drive of 'the world' is to 'get your own back'; 'I'm entitled to compensation'; 'an eye for an eye – it's only fair'; and, in school, 'I told him, if he hits him again, to hit him back'; 'I want that teacher punished: he can't do that to my child and get away with it'. Our Church schools must work to stem the tide; if our communities show forgiveness, then our children will learn forgiveness. Again, I do not pretend that is easy, dilemmas abound: how can we maintain discipline? What about standards?

FOR DISCUSSION:

1. *Can we maintain discipline and yet continue to be a forgiving community?*

2. *How can we deal with an unforgiving parent?*

3. *How can we better show compassion?*

The specific dilemma of how to tie together discipline and forgiveness is not new. It must be a central element in the life of every family, or at least those which do seek to take forgiveness seriously. Of course, there are significant differences to be borne in mind when considering the same matter in our schools. Families are, by their very nature, small and intimate. In such groupings the relationships will be qualitatively different from those in the larger school community. One would hope, at least, that within families there is such an 'accumulation' of love, that when parental discipline is needed, it can be exerted in such a way that relationships will not be lastingly damaged. Of course, that will not always be the case; although many of us will have come across situations in which, although parents are treating their child abysmally, the love of the child for the parents is steadfast. This kind of love is pre-eminently a function of hope. There is, however, bound to be some sense in which the use of punishment in the larger, less intimate school community has the potential to be that little more destructive of relationships. Furthermore, in the larger school community, the adult has the fundamental problem not found (or not found so acutely) in families: the need *pour encourager les autres*. When, in our schools, we are dealing with breaches of discipline, it is not simply the needs of the individual child which we must consider, it is the needs of the whole community. In this situation discipline and forgiveness become particularly problematic. Yes, we do recognize the reasons why this child has done such a dreadful thing; yes, we do want to be able to reflect forgiveness and love on our response. But how will the other children see it? Will they regard our efforts and forgiveness as weakness? Will they think, not knowing the whole story: 'Well, if he can get away with it...'

As we are seeking rather more to raise questions on which a school might wish to reflect than to provide easy (?) answers, it will suffice simply to draw colleagues' attention to a collection of essays in the second edition of the Journal of the Association of Anglican Secondary School Heads, in which several practitioners wrestle with these difficult issues, which, I suggest, are far more difficult in our Church schools than in any other.[1] In our reflections, however, we may find it helpful to consider the relationship between God and the Jews in the Jewish scriptures. Very often the 'children of Israel' are portrayed as erring children, who need disciplining in order to return to the 'straight and narrow'. Perhaps the most direct example of this is the prophecy of Hosea, used by St Matthew as one of the 'proof texts' of his Christmas story:

> When Israel was a boy, I loved him; I called my son out of
> Egypt; but the more I called, the further they went from
> me. It was I who taught Ephraim to walk, I who had
> taken them in my arms; but they did not know that I har-
> nessed them in leading-strings and led them with bonds of
> love. Back they shall go to Egypt, the Assyrian shall be
> their king; for they refused to return to me.[2]

Here we have God punishing his people, like punishing a
wayward child, because they have turned from him, and gone 'a
whoring after [other] gods'.[3] (An even more intriguing model,
also used by Hosea, is that of the faithless wife.) So his anger is
directed towards them, and they are duly punished. But the
problem went on. Time and time again Israel was 'naughty' and
time and again, s/he was dealt with. God is like a parent, or a
teacher, in despair:

> O Ephraim, how shall I deal with you? How shall I deal
> with you, Judah? Your loyalty to me is like the morning
> mist, like dew that vanishes early. Therefore have I lashed
> you through the prophets and torn you to shreds with my
> words.[4]

That is, of course, not the end of the story. There have been those,
like Marcion in the second century, who have wanted to differen-
tiate between the 'God of the Old Testament' – an allegedly
vengeful God – and the 'God and Father of our Lord Jesus
Christ', as being totally different. But that is simply to misunder-
stand the Old Testament. As well as the very strong sense of God
disciplining his people, there is always an equal or greater emphasis on his constant forgiveness.

This, indeed, is part of God's very nature, 'As a father has compassion on his children, so has the Lord compassion on all who
fear him. For he knows how we were made.'[5]

Our reflections have, at last, led us to the central value – the
nature of God himself – which lies behind forgiveness, and which

will, inevitably lead us to reconciliation: the Hebrew term is '*hesed*', and we can pick it up concluding the quotation from Hosea 6 above (now from the Revised Standard Version), 'For I desire steadfast love ['*hesed*'] and not sacrifice, the knowledge of God, rather than burnt offerings.'[6]

'*Hesed*' is a very difficult term to translate into English, and different versions of the Bible have approached it variously: 'mercy' (AV), 'loyalty' (NEB), 'goodness' (American Jewish Translation). Although here it is God who requires '*hesed*' from Israel, the term is more usually the quality (or value) that a superior shows to an inferior (Jonathan to David at first, and then when David's star appears to be rising, Jonathan wants it from David.[7]) But we may confirm that '*hesed*' is the very nature of God by considering that remarkable passage where Moses has made the very audacious request that he be allowed to see God's glory. Because no-one can directly experience God and live, God allows him to see his back!

> The Lord passed before him and proclaimed, 'The Lord, the Lord, a God merciful and gracious, slow to anger, and abounding in steadfast love ['*hesed*'] and faithfulness, keeping steadfast love for thousands, forgiving iniquity and transgression and sin, but who will by no means clear the guilty.'[8]

This, then, may be considered to be an important clue to the proper nature of the Christian adult (parent or teacher) relationship with the child. It obviously does not preclude discipline and punishment, but it will dictate the manner in which they are exercised.

We may go further, as we move from the Old to the New Testament. At the centre of our faith lies that great affirmation of St John, 'And the Word became flesh and dwelt among us, full of grace and truth.'[9] Both this, and that of Moses (above), are to be seen as revelatory experiences and, as Anthony Hanson points out, revelations of the same 'Thou':

The Hebrew [for 'abounding in steadfast love and faith-fulness'] consists of only three words: *'rab hesed we'emeth'*. This is precisely rendered in John 1.14 with *'pleres kharitos kai aletheias'*. Our familiar translation 'full of grace and truth' tends rather to divert attention from the fact that this is a quotation from Exodus 34.6, since *'hesed'* is not normally rendered with 'grace'. But John's word *'kharis'* in fact is occasionally used in the LXX [Septuagint – Greek translation of the Old Testament] as a translation of *'hesed'*... [John's] intention is clear: the same God who showed himself to Moses... has now manifested himself in Jesus Christ and can be recognised as manifesting the same essential characteristics, grace and truth, or better still love and faithfulness.[10]

It is, therefore, God who corrects his children. With compassion, yes, but he does correct them and disciplines them. But this is the God revealed by Jesus Christ as the One who is always willing to forgive. This is the simple message of the prodigal son, which, nevertheless, takes us even further: the father did not wait for his son to come grovelling to him; he was sitting and awaiting his return (we may imagine, pacing around, glancing at the horizon), and when he saw his son in the distance, 'While he was still a long way off... his heart went out to him. He ran to meet him, flung his arms around him, and kissed him.'[11]

This wonderful icon is replicated in the, sadly less often used, post-communion prayer of Rite A:

'Father of all, we give you thanks and praise, that when we were still far off you met us in your Son and brought us home.'[12]

If our schools are truly eucharistic (thanking) communities, then that must determine our attitude towards the disciplining of our pupils. Which does not to make it any easier to put into practice.

Reconciliation

... God was in Christ reconciling the world to himself, no longer holding men's misdeeds against them, and... he has entrusted us with the message of reconciliation. (2 Corinthians 5.19)

FOR DISCUSSION:

1. *How effective is the anti-bullying policy? Does it enable true reconciliation?*

2. *What should the Church school do with an incompetent teacher?*

3. *Is our governing body a vehicle of reconciliation?*

For St Paul, reconciliation was the full and sufficient reason why 'God was in Christ' and, as he pointed out explicitly, we are called to share in that ministry of reconciliation.[1] Our communities must, therefore, be communities of reconciliation, and reconciliation presupposes the giving *and* acceptance of forgiveness. In the secular world, forgiveness and reconciliation often seem to be seen simply as displays of weakness.

But forgiveness needs to be accompanied by reconciliation. We might now consider a slightly different model: what might be done in our school communities to reconcile the bully and victim. The same principles apply to this imperative, but here the emphasis will be on inter-pupil relationships, rather than those between pupils and teacher. But then, we may remind ourselves, our vocation is to spread the 'message of reconciliation'.[2] If God, in Christ, no longer holds our misdeeds against us, and we are his ambassadors, then what more can we do but seek to promote reconciliation in our school communities.

Of course, it must be taken for granted that the bully, in order to receive forgiveness, must repent (the prodigal son had to make the journey home in the first place). That, as many of us have experienced, is often the easier part! The act of bullying is destructive, and the victim may have been deeply scarred by it. Neither may his/her parents be 'the forgiving sort'; many of us come time and again against a lynch-mob mentality. In returning to Hosea, we may both consolidate forgiveness and reconciliation and be led on to the greatest value of them all. Hosea was quite damning and frightening in his condemnations: God is compared even with a wild animal that pounces on human prey,[3] to a moth or dry rot that destroys the fabric of society.[4] Indeed God will 'love them no more'.[5]

And yet (again!), the depth of God's love cannot be plumbed, 'I will not let loose my fury, I will not turn round and destroy Ephraim; for I am God and not a man, the Holy One in your midst.'[6]

'*Hesed*' prevails; even to the Cross.[7] Reconciliation is established as an essential value for any Christian community. The fact that there are Christian communities (not only in Northern Ireland), which cannot grasp this, only shames us all.

Justice

But let justice roll down like waters, and righteousness
like an everflowing stream. (Amos 5.24)

FOR DISCUSSION:

1. *Would you consider your school community to be a just
   one? What are the hallmarks of justice to be found in it?*

2. *Just what is our role in God's plan of salvation?*

3. *Does the school manage to treat pupils as individuals
   according to their needs?*

4. *Does our school confuse 'equality of opportunity' with
   equality of treatment?*

The context of this saying of the prophet Amos is important. He
has been castigating Israel for complacency and arrogance. The
people have been expecting the coming 'Day of the Lord' to be
party-time. After all, God was on their side, wasn't he? But no!

> I hate, I despise your festivals, and I take no delight in
> your solemn assemblies. Even though you offer me your
> burnt offerings and grain offerings, I will not accept them;
> and the offerings of well-being of your fatted animals I
> will not look upon. Take away from me the noise of your
> songs; I will not listen to the melody of your harps. But...[1]

We might consider this to be a salutary message for our churches
today, with our preoccupation with liturgical minutiae and doc-
trinal hair-splitting. The more important value is simply – justice.
But how may justice be found? What are the issues that affect our
Church schools?

Despite Amos, 'justice' is a rare biblical word, and doesn't appear at all in the New Testament, except as '*dike*', meaning retributive justice.[2] Nevertheless, its intention, as portrayed by Amos, must surely make it a Christian value. One value which is linked fundamentally not only to judgement, but intrinsically to forgiveness and reconciliation as well. In the Hebrew, '*tsedeq*' and '*tsedaqah*' may be translated both as justice and righteousness, and these (like 'steadfast love and faithfulness') are divine characteristics. When God judges, he judges righteously, and the experience of the people of the Bible is that this involves a substantial 'slice' of mercy/'*hesed*' (the Vulgate translation as '*justitia*' connotes compassion and clemency). In other words, it is not just a description of God's behaviour (the moral dimension, again) but a function of his will to save. Whenever these words are used, however, they are tied into God's concern for the poor and needy, over against the powerful. They emphasize what John Hull has called a 'magnificat theology' for Church schools.[3] In the context of our school communities, they might alternatively be described as 'equal opportunity' words.

Our schools will have equal opportunity policies. Many of these will, no doubt, have secular origins. That doesn't make them poor policies, but do they succeed in reflecting the value of justice in its Biblical sense? How far, for example, do we offer equality of opportunity, while we forget that the particular needs of people may require them to be treated differently? Schools will, no doubt, be considering this in the light of female career opportunities. Do we really manage to treat children as individuals according to their needs? Do we operate policy bias that enables us to 'lift up the lowly'?[4] The whole point about justice, connoting elements of judgement and mercy, is that it is not an end in itself, but an element in God's plan of salvation.[5] Our Church schools also have their role to play in this plan!

Peace

Jesus came and stood among them and said, 'Peace be with you'. (John 20.19b)

FOR DISCUSSION:

1. *In what circumstances are we called upon to bring peace; and how is this best done?*

2. *'Shalom'. Is our school community peaceful?*

3. *How can we present Jesus to our pupils as someone with whom they can really relate?*

The twentieth century has seen the rise of many peace movements which in the 1920s and 1930s were focused on the League of Nations, and had a significant effect on the British Government's policy of appeasement. In the 1950s and beyond, they were centred much on CND, and the anti-nuclear lobby. History will make its own judgements on such movements in terms of what they achieved. The earlier movement has been criticised for helping to create a situation where war actually became more likely, because the overwhelming desire for peace, 'at any cost', led to pressure to treat with Hitler, and delayed rearmament. It is probably too early to judge just how much influence the latter movement has had in bringing about a situation in which the threat of nuclear war has diminished. But whatever judgements may be made, it is the case that both movements were fundamentally negative in that they were against something. True, it was war which they were against, and we thank God for that (the last thing I want to do is to decry either their commitment or their striving to end war, not least because I have been a part of it; the outlawing of war is an entirely laudable aim[1]). But as a result, in the popular mind, peace simply equates to the absence of war. It is much more than this.

'*Eirene*' is a positive term. Linked with healing, it connotes a wholeness that is far more than simply the cessation of fighting, however important that is in itself. Certainly it is sometimes easier to understand peace in terms of its opposite, 'We usually think of war... as the opposite of peace, but wherever human life is fractured, peace has been destroyed.'[2] If peace is destroyed by the fracturing of human life, then peace (as we shall see) is an aspect of healing. The fracture is mended. A much more helpful concept is mediated by the Hebrew '*Shalom*':

> a comprehensive word, covering the manifold relationships of daily life. Fundamental meaning is 'totality'... 'well-being', 'harmony', with stress on material prosperity untouched by violence or misfortune... the normal and proper condition of men in relationship with one another, enjoyed most intimately in the family.[3]

We say in our eucharistic liturgy: 'Christ is our Peace'.[4] As part of the daily courtesies of life, Jesus would have greeted people with '*Shalom*'; and so especially he greeted his close friends after the resurrection.[5] So it is he who is the bringer of well-being and harmony into our lives. We may tie this into our understanding of atonement. Being 'at one' with God is the aim and purpose of our lives. There have been many 'theories of atonement' – substitutionary, ransom, exemplary, etc. All of these have been to a greater or lesser extent unsatisfactory, because they have tended to be somewhat narrow in their focus. Some may have wondered how we could come so far in our reflections, particularly having passed through 'judgement', without mentioning 'sin'. So here we are!

The bringer of atonement is 'the Lamb of God who takes away the sin of the world'.[6] How Jesus may be understood to do this is usually, and somewhat haltingly, approached via the doctrine of the 'sinlessness of Christ'. Only he who is without sin can bring salvation from sin.[7] The problem is that this notion means little today. It is difficult in a scientific age to go along with Augustine in seeing 'original sin' being transmitted via the male sperm (hence needing virginal conception; but that is another matter!). It is also problematic seeing the real Jesus as a 'goody-two-shoes' – how many times have children been told that, as a child, Jesus never did anything wrong, that he was never naughty? So they must be like him.[8] In the same breath, he also becomes quite irrelevant, being in this sense not a bit like us, nor related to our experience of real life. There is an alternative way of understanding sinlessness. It is:

> the end of a process of development. Sin itself is a negative – a disorder and separation from God; sinlessness is in turn the negation of the negativity of sin... the disorder is overcome and... the separation from God is replaced by a coming together of God and man... sinlessness describes an aspect of christhood.[9]

So we may understand sin, analogically, as a *breakdown, fracture* or even *blockage* of and in our relationship with God. Then Jesus Christ is, respectively, the divine AA man, orthopaedic surgeon or plumber who brings his peace. Alternatively, Jesus is the Second Adam who reverses the sin of disobedience through obedience 'even to death on the cross',[10] and so enables us all to approach God as his brothers and sisters.

But if we value peace, and who would not, then we must strive that our schools are instruments of peace, sharers in and mediators of Christ's gift of atonement. On the one level, St Francis of Assisi has it all worked out for us,[11] but beyond this our understanding of peace must say things to us about the very nature of our communities. Are they really peace-full communities? Is this what is perceived by those who belong, and those who visit? Do harmony and well-being reign?

Healing

> And wherever he went, into villages or cities or farms, they laid the sick in the market places, and begged him that they might touch even the fringe of his cloak, and all who touched it were healed. (Mark 6.56)

FOR DISCUSSION:

1. *How can our school community bring healing and wholeness to pupils who have been damaged by their lives at home? What are the implications for home–school relationships?*

2. *In what sense might a family find salvation/healing in our school?*

3. *Is our concern to eradicate ignorance as part of the healing process?*

4. *As Christian teachers and governors, how can we learn to accept healing ourselves?*

Healing is salvation. The Greek '*soteria*' translates both. There is a real sense in which all the great religions are systems of salvation. That is their simple purpose, 'they all recognise... that ordinary human existence is defective, unsatisfactory, lacking... suffering, insecurity and mortality [are thought of] in terms implying a contrast with something fundamentally different.'[1]

It is this difference – that we call salvation or healing – which, in our Christian tradition, is also known as redemption and eternal life. Human life is, therefore, in a condition of disorder. To the Christian (as we have just seen) it is full of sin which requires atonement. To the Hindu it is lost in '*avidya*', ignorance which longs for the liberating force of truth. These values become more and more complementary. Together the combined pictures of disobedience and ignorance pierce to the root of the human condition, and the only prescription is healing. If, for a moment more, we stay with the Christian–Hindu 'connection', we may find helpful the words of Abhishiktananda, the Roman Catholic monk (birth name: Henri Le Saux), who lived much of his Christian life amongst Hindus:

> [Jesus is] the Guru who imparted a new dynamic to the life of men, by beginning a process of reorientating their imaginations, by opening their eyes... he brought into human life a new Being, a new Consciousness, a new Bliss.[2]

Being/'*sat*', consciousness/'*cit*' and bliss/'*ananda*' have sometimes been compared to the Christian understanding of God as Trinity. While this is probably pressing the matter too far, it is a hint that however healing comes, its origin is God. Sometimes our symbols and structures may appear to be contradictory rather than complementary, but then this happens not only between faiths, but within them as well. We can also learn from each other, for example:

> the Indian emphasis on an original ignorance is a good corrective to the unrealistic moralism of the all-too-prevalent interpretation of the Adam myth. If we look at the life of man we see that the many choices made are as much due to ignorance and lack of imagination as to defects of the will.[3]

If we stop to think for a moment we can see just how true this is. The whole thrust of this booklet has been to attempt to locate morality in a much wider context. Yes! Our wills are defective; we only too often make the wrong decisions and do the wrong things 'through negligence, through weakness, through our own deliberate fault'.[4] But do we not also suffer from a great lack of imagination, in that we seek to confine God to our notions of what he should

75

be like, rather than opening ourselves to the penetration of his Being. Do we not spend too much of our energy seeking to share our ignorance with others, instead of enlightening our own minds with their insights? Especially if the authors of those insights are children!

So how far do our schools provide healing? In asking this question we move inexorably towards the pinnacle of our Christian values system. Before we do so, we should learn to take most seriously the fact that we ourselves need to accept healing, and that within our school communities we may even find it.

Agape

In a word, there are three things that last forever: faith, hope and love; but the greatest of them all is love. (1 Corinthians 13.13)

> FOR DISCUSSION:
>
> 1. Can our community teach children to love sacrificially? How?
>
> 2. Is our governing body a model of agape (Christian love)?
>
> 3. Would an outsider 'know we are Christians by our love'?
>
> 4. How far can we, or should we, compensate for lack of parental love?
>
> 5. Is our school a servant community?

It seems almost trite to say that our Church schools should be agapeistic, if only because *'agape'* is too easily trivialized ('love is'). It is a frightening value! True love is totally unselfish, totally self-giving; love empowers the beloved, and may weaken the lover. How one interprets this sort of value into the lives of our communities, which are earthenware jars, is a continuing dilemma. But interpret it we must. Needless to say that, properly interpreted, we are dealing here with what St Paul called the greatest of gifts, what we might, therefore, call the greatest value. As that, it must infuse the very life of our Church schools, it must dictate every action, and inform every relationship. As the greatest, it is also the most difficult, for it lies at the root of all other values, and they depend on it.

The exemplar of love is Jesus. We may understand that love was of his essence, just as it is of the essence of God himself,[1] and that it was this above all else which constituted the raising of humanity to divinity. As we know in our own lives, at least in part, it is love that enables the beloved to be most truly him/herself. This is because the person (so-to-speak) 'in receipt' of love, has been so empowered by that love that nothing can overcome it. This, St Paul tells us, is how God's love is to be understood.[2]

But love is a funny thing! We may think we are giving it when, in fact, we are doing precisely the opposite. In the words of the children's hymn: 'Love is something if you give it away... you end up having more.'[3] But imagine the parent who so loves his child that he does not want to lose the child – ever. That is understandable; but it is not love. It is, in fact, a perversion of it. Love must be prepared to let go. Unless the parent allows the child to be him/herself, the potentiality in that particular human being can never be realized. In fact the child–parent relationship is a very good model. It is only when the parent lets go that they can both find a new, more mature, more certain kind of love. This is the love that enables us to have a new perception of the child, perhaps even as partners who bask in the love of God who 'becomes the third party in every relationship of love'.[4]

In a sense true '*agape*' is the vocation of a challenge for the whole of humanity. We may understand it in terms of moving out from

ourselves (being led out?) towards a love in which we put ourselves last; simply unselfishness. A baby is totally and naturally (is
this what we mean by original sin?) self-centred; it screams when
it is hot, when it is cold, when it is wet, when it is hungry. Unless
everything is absolutely geared for its comfort, it can be horrendous! I use extravagant language just to make the point. So what
happens as the baby grows up? It learns that it is not the centre
of the universe, that there are others whose needs are just as,
perhaps even more, important. At least it should! But we know
that there are those who never really move far away from self,
and, even more regrettably, appear to move very quickly back to
that baby state in old age. Our Christian faith calls us to leave self
behind entirely: 'whoever wants to be great must be your
servant'.[5] Only when we lose ourselves can we truly find God.
Can we imagine the unimaginable: that we weren't born – what a
horrendous thought, that the world may have been deprived of
us! Of course, we can be just as selfish for our own as we are for
ourselves. Consider the Sunday School party when all one of the
'mum-helpers' does is ensure that her child is being looked after.
There are other contexts in which there is nothing more frighten-
ingly selfish than tribal or family 'loyalty'.

The implications for our school communities are enormous. We
may only consider some here. What are we to do with the
children whose parental love is lacking or perverse? Can we show
something of the love of God to them? How can this be done in
such a way as to build up, rather than break down, the home
relationships? What of the teacher–pupil relationship, particularly
when the teacher is not an icon of love? How does the Christian
community itself show the love of God in the inter-personal
relationships between staff? And what of outside perceptions –
when people visit the school are they struck by such an ethos, that
'they'll know we are Christians by our love'?[6] We should believe
that as the love of God works on our lives, so those lives can be
transformed by it, and in their turn radiate that love to others.
Here may lie our ultimate distinctiveness.

Notes

Preface

[1]   Ecclesiastes 3.7

What is a value?

[1]   The study, or theory, of value is known as 'axiology', from the Greek 'axios', meaning 'worthy'.

[2]   J. Macquarrie (ed.), *Dictionary of Christian Ethics*, SCM Press, 1967, p. 352.

[3]   I. Murdoch, *The Sovereignty of Good*, Routledge & Kegan Paul, 1970, pp. 58, 8.

[4]   albeit making 'oversimplified interpretations of Nietzsche's sermons', J.C. Fest, *Hitler*, E.T. Weidenfeld and Nicolson, 1974, p. 56.

[5]   D. Cupitt, *The New Christian Ethics*, SCM, 1988, pp. 43–44.

The problem with values

[1]   For John's Gospel *ho kosmos* is the world of human affairs contrasted with 'the world above' (John 8.23).

[2]   R.C. Solomon and K.M. Higgins, *A Short History of Philosophy*, Oxford University Press, 1996, p. 243.

[3]   Smith, in Macquarrie, *Dictionary*, p. 352.

Can we speak of 'foundation values'?

[1]   Now the Qualifications and Curriculum Authority (QCA).

[2]   *The Times*, 10 April 1997.

[3]   *The Times*, 11 April 1997.

[4]   My italics: an article on the National Forum for Values in Education and the Community, in SCAA's own newsletter, *Inform*, July 1997, was headed simply 'Moral Values'.

[5]   My italics: now commonly designated SMSC.

[6]   For example, various headlines in *The Times Educational Supplement*, 1 November 1996: 'SCAA shows a way back to goodness', 'Believer in moral truth comes into her own', 'Whose morals are they anyway?' etc.

[7]   *Church Times*, 1 November 1996.

[8]   'By being so connected with the actual covenant relationship, law itself could be seen as part of God's blessing.' A. Phillips, *God BC*, Oxford University Press, 1977, p. 2.

[9]   Exodus 32.1-14

[10]   J.J. Kupperman, 'Axiological Ethics', in T. Honderich (ed.), *The Oxford Companion to Philosophy*, Oxford University Press, 1995, p. 71.

[11]   *The Times*, 25 October 1996.

[12]   'Christ is our cornerstone', trans. J. Chandler, 1937.

[13]   Cupitt, *New Christian Ethics*, p. 51ff: For Cupitt this is essentially about 'remaking the Christian self' and 'remaking Christian action'. A similar exercise might be carried out using Humanist principles.

[14]   Cupitt would presumably argue that nothing can precede them, because they are the givens by which we interpret our existence: 'value is there already', *New Christian Ethics*, p. 44.

The search for the holy grail

[1]   The SCAA Briefing Note, March 1997, tells us that 'spiritual' is 'concerned with... ultimate values'.

[2]   OFSTED *Guidance on the Inspection of Secondary Schools*, 1996, p. 88 seems to imply that values and beliefs are exactly the same thing.

[3]   'Teaching not just facts, but values', *Church Times*, 3 October 1997.

[4]   'Teaching not just facts, but values', *Church Times*, 3 October 1997.

[5]   e.g. *awe* is given short shrift!

What of Anglican Schools?

[1]   John 1.10-11

[2]   John 8.48

[3]   John 16.33

The importance of 'God-talk'

[1]   Evagrius Ponticus (AD 345–399), *De Oratione*, 60.

[2]   W. Thompson, *Christology and Spirituality*, Crossroad, 1991, pp. xi–xii (my italics).

3   Psalm 46.10

4   J. Eaton, *The Contemplative Face of Old Testament Wisdom*, SCM Press, 1989, p. 132.

5   Ecclesiastes 3.7b

6   Thompson, *Christology and Spirituality*, p. xii.

7   John 3.8

On the values journey

1   1 Corinthians 11.23; 15.3

2   e.g. eucharistic worship is based 'solely on tradition'. G. Dix, *The Shape of the Liturgy*, Dacre Press, 1943, p. 3.

3   J.F. Jungmann, *The Place of Christ in Liturgical Prayer*, 1925, Chapman, (pub. 1989), p. xvii.

4   'revelation... on pain of becoming manifest as superstition [must] vindicate its claim by satisfying reason.' W. Temple, *Nature, Men and God*, Macmillan, 1940, p. 396.

5   Revelation 4.11 (New English Bible)

Christian values within the curriculum

Awe, wonder and fascination

1   Edgar Mitchell, Apollo 14 Astronaut, quoted in K. Kelley, *The Home Planet*, Macdonald, 1988, Photographs pp. 42–45.

2   Kelley's book is dedicated 'to all the children of the world'.

3   R. Otto, *Idea of the Holy*, p. 22.

4   Rex Ambler, 'Where on earth is God?' in F. Young (ed.), *Dare we Speak of God in Public?*, Mowbray, 1995, p. 94.

5   Mark 4.11; Matthew 16.17; Ephesians 6.19

6   J. Hick, *The Metaphor of God Incarnate*, SCM Press, 1993, p. 164.

7   A. Cohen, *The Tremendum*, Crossroads, 1981, pp. 34–35.

8   Chapter title in Rubenstein and Roth, *Approaches to Auschwitz*, SCM Press, 1987.

9   Richard Jeffries (1848–1887), *The Story of my Heart*, Longman, 1907, p. 38.

Humility

[1] Stephen Hawking, *A Brief History of Time*, Bantam Press, 1988.

[2] Paul Davies, *The Mind of God*, Simon and Schuster, 1992, pp. 14–15.

[3] Job 38.4. Obviously the issues are much more complex, as explored by Muriel Spark in her fascinating novel, *The Only Problem*, 1984: 'God as a character comes out very badly. Thunder and bluster and I'm Me, who are you?... And Job insincerely and wrongly says "I am vile".' in *Muriel Spark Omnibus* 1, Constable, 1993, p. 310.

[4] 'Education' properly stems from the Latin '*educare*', 'to train'; but I prefer to think of it, quite wrongly I confess, as coming from '*educere*', meaning 'to lead out'. It allows the development of a much richer sequence of ideas.

[5] The distinction can be traced to Plato; for the Greeks *phusis*, 'nature', connoted emergence and development, and so it is our human nature to 'emerge' towards our potentiality; however, I am aware that, in strict philosophical terms, my contrast between 'being' and 'becoming' is rather too simplistic. For a much fuller discussion, see J. Macquarrie, *Principles of Christian Theology*, SCM Press, 1977, p. 222ff and D. Cupitt, *The Last Philosophy*, SCM Press, 1995, p. 144.

Concern for the truth

[1] Francis Bacon, *Essays*, 'Of Truth', 1625.

[2] John 1.14

[3] John 14.6. See also John 15.26

[4] V. Mehta, *Mahatma Gandhi and his Apostles*, Penguin Books, 1976, pp. 161–162.

[5] John 8.44

[6] Luke 12.10

[7] G.B. Caird, *St Luke*, Penguin Books, 1976, pp. 161.

[8] C.S. Lewis, *The Great Divorce*, Collins, 1946, p. 41.

[9] Jeremiah 1.10

Possibility

[1] James Russell Lowell (1819–1891), *The Present Crisis*.

Rationality

[1] D. Adams, *The Hitch-Hikers Guide to the Galaxy*, Pan Books, 1979, p. 136.

[2] John 1.1

[3] Genesis 1.3,6,9,11,14,20,24,26

[4] St Athanasius, *De Incarnatione*, liv 3.

[5] Theophilus of Antioch, *Ad Autolycum*, II.24.

[6] Macquarrie, *Principles*, p. 300.

[7] For Anthony Hanson '[God] has chosen to express himself through the form of man. He is the anthropomorphic God'. *The Image of the Invisible God*, SCM, 1982, p. 127.

[8] Hebrews 1.3

[9] A.M. Ramsey, *God, Christ and the World*, SCM, 1969, p. 98.

[10] J.A.T. Robinson, *The Roots of a Radical*, SCM, 1980, pp. 61–62.

[11] Quoted by St Augustine in *The City of God*, xix. 23 (my italics).

Responsibility

[1] Matthew 25.14-30; Luke 16.1-9 and 12.35-40 may be interestingly juxtaposed.

Hope

[1] 'Abandon all hope, you who enter!', Dante, *Divine Comedy*, Inferno, Canto 3,1.1.

[2] Prayer of St Francis of Assisi.

[3] L.P. Hartley, *The Go-Between*, Penguin Books, 1953, p. 7.

[4] Thomas Richard, *Star Trek in Myth and Legend*, Orion Books, 1997, p. 142.

[5] Doctrine Commission of the Church of England, Church House Publishing, 1995, p. 200.

Risk

[1] John Hick, *Evil and the God of Love*, Macmillan, London, & New York, 1985, (first published 1966).

[2] I. Trethowan, *Mysticism and Theology*, Geoffrey Chapman, London, 1975, p. 32.

3   Macquarrie, *Principles*, p. 51.
4   John Hick, *An Interpretation of Religion*, Macmillan, London & New York, 1989, p. 360.

Christian values within the school community

A sacramental universe

1   J. Macquarrie, *A Guide to the Sacraments*, SCM Press, 1997, p. 1.
2   Galatians 5.17
3   W. Spens, 'The Eucharist', in (ed.) E.C. Selwyn, *Essays Catholic and Crictical*, SPCK, 1926, p. 441.

Signs and symbols of transcendence

1   F.W. Dillistone, *The Power of Symbols*, SCM Press, 1986, p. 219.
2   Psalm 51.1,9-10

Relationship

1   M. Buber, *I and Thou*, (trans. R.G. Smith) T.&T. Clark, 1937.
2   Feuerbach, *The Essence of Christianity*, (trans. Evans) Harper Torchbooks, 1957, p. 92.
3   Frances Young, 'Dare we mention prayer?' in *Dare we Speak of God in Public?*, Mowbray, 1995, p. 145.
4   F. Young, as above, p. 147.

Faith

1   E. Burns (b. 1938), various hymnbooks
2   Lewis Carroll, *Alice's Adventures in Wonderland* and *Through the Looking Glass*, OUP, 1971, p. 177.
3   'Not necessary'– we and our universe might not have been!
4   Bernhard Anderson, *The Living World of the Old Testament*, Longman, 4th ed. pp. 170–1.

Commitment

1   W.M. Abbott (ed.), *Documents of Vatican II*, Chapman, 1966, pp. 661–662.

² J. Hick, *God and the Universe of Faiths*, Collins, 1977, p. 131.

³ J. Hick, 'Is there only one way to God?', *Theology*, January 1982, p. 4.

⁴ Hick, *Universe*, p. 102.

⁵ Alice Meynell (1847–1922), *Christ in the Universe*. See also the speculative essay by W.B. Easton, Life on Other Planets, in I. Barbour (ed.), *Science and Religion*, SCM, 1968, and also a whole range of Sci-Fi novels, exploring the same theme, e.g. James Blish, *A Case of Conscience*.

⁶ J. Macquarrie, *Theology, Church and Ministry*, SCM, 1986, p. 150.

⁷ John 8.12

Acceptance

¹ C.F. Alexander (1818–1848), *All things bright and beautiful*.

² Cromwell actually said: 'Warts and everything'.

³ 2 Peter 3.18

⁴ *The Alternative Service Book 1980*, p. 248.

⁵ *The Alternative Service Book 1980*, p. 243.

⁶ Macquarrie, *Principles*, p. 345.

Grace

¹ St Thomas Aquinas, *Summa Theologiae*, 1a, 1, 8.

² 1 Corinthians 15.10

³ D.M. Baillie, *God was in Christ*, Faber, 1948, p. 114.

⁴ Mark 8.35

⁵ Meister Eckhart, (1260–1327) *Tractates*, XIX.

⁶ DfEE, *Framework for the Reorganisation of Schools*, Technical Consultation Paper, August 1997.

Judgement

¹ John 5.24; 12.31; 14.16

² John 3.17; see also, John 3.18; 5.24

³ C.K. Barrett, *The Gospel According to St John*, SPCK, (2nd ed.) 1978, pp. 217–218.

⁴ M. Hinton, *Comprehensive Schools: A Christian's View*, SCM, 1979, p. 14.

⁵ Macquarrie, *Principles*, p. 353.

Forgiveness

1   *Managing a Christian School*, AASSH, April 1997; see particularly articles by Peter Crook and Dick Williams.
2   Hosea 11.1-5
3   Exodus 34.15 (Authorised Version)
4   Hosea 6.4-5
5   Psalm 103.13-14
6   Hosea 6.6 (Revised Standard Version)
7   1 Samuel 20.8a; then 1 Samuel 20.12-17
8   Exodus 34.6-7, (Revised Standard Version)
9   John 1.14
10 A.T. Hanson, *Grace and Truth – A Study in the Doctrine of the Incarnation*, SPCK, 1975, p. 6.
11 Luke 15.20
12 *The Alternative Service Book 1980*, p. 144.

Reconciliation

1   2 Corinthians 5.18-20
2   2 Corinthians 5.18:20
3   Hosea 5.14; 13.7-8
4   Hosea 5.12
5   Hosea 9.15
6   Hosea 11.9
7   Luke 23.34

Justice

1   Amos 5.21-23
2   e.g. Acts 28.4
3   Lecture at the Annual Conference of AASSH 1991.
4   Luke 1.52
5   Isaiah 45.8

Peace

1 Micah 4.3
2 J. Macquarrie, *The Concept of Peace*, SCM Press, 1973, p. 5.
3 C.F. Evans, in A. Richardson (ed.), *Theological Word Book of the Bible*, SCM Press, 1950, p. 165.
4 'The Peace', Rite A, *The Alternative Service Book 1980*, p. 128.
5 John 20.19
6 John 1.29
7 Hebrews 4.15
8 'Mild, obedient, good as he', from 'Once in Royal David's City'.
9 Macquarrie, *Principles*, p. 301.
10 Philippians 2.8
11 'Where there is hatred', Prayer of St. Francis.

Healing

1 J. Hick, *An Interpretation of Religion*, pp. 32–33.
2 H. Le Saux, *Saccidananda*, ISPCK, 1984, pp. 165–166.
3 N. Smart, *The Yogi and the Devotee*, Allen & Unwin, 1968, p. 158.
4 Prayer of Confession, *The Alternative Service Book 1980*, p. 127.

Agape

1 1 John 4.9
2 Romans 8.38-39
3 Malvina Reynolds, *The Magic Penny*, Northern Music, USA, 1955.
4 Kierkegaard, *Works of Love*, 1847, (tr. Swenson, 1946), p. 124.
5 Mark 10.43
6 Peter Scholtes, *We are One in the Spirit*, F.E.L Pubs, Los Angeles.

The National Society
A Christian Voice in Education

The National Society (Church of England) for Promoting Religious Education supports everyone involved in Christian education – teachers, school governors, students, parents, clergy, parish and diocesan education teams – with the resources of its RE centres, courses, conferences and archives.

Founded in 1811, the Society was chiefly responsible for setting up the nationwide network of Church schools in England and Wales, and still helps them with legal and administrative advice for headteachers and governors. It was also a pioneer in teacher education through the Church colleges. The Society now provides resources for those responsible for RE and worship in any school, lecturers and students in colleges, and clergy and lay people in parish education. It publishes a wide range of books and booklets and a resource magazine, *Together with Children*.

The National Society is a voluntary body which works in partnership with the Church of England General Synod Board of Education and the Division for Education of the Church of Wales. An Anglican society, it also operates ecumenically, and helps to promote inter-faith education and dialogue through its RE centres.

For further details of the Society or a copy of our current resources catalogue and how you can support the continuing work of the Society, please contact:

The National Society
Church House
Great Smith Street
London SW1P 3NZ

Telephone: 0171-222 1672
Fax: 0171-233 2592
Email: NS@natsoc.org.uk